THE ATLAS OF THE OCEANS

Linda Sonntag

Consultant: Professor Trevor A Norton

Copper Beech Books
Brookfield, Connecticut

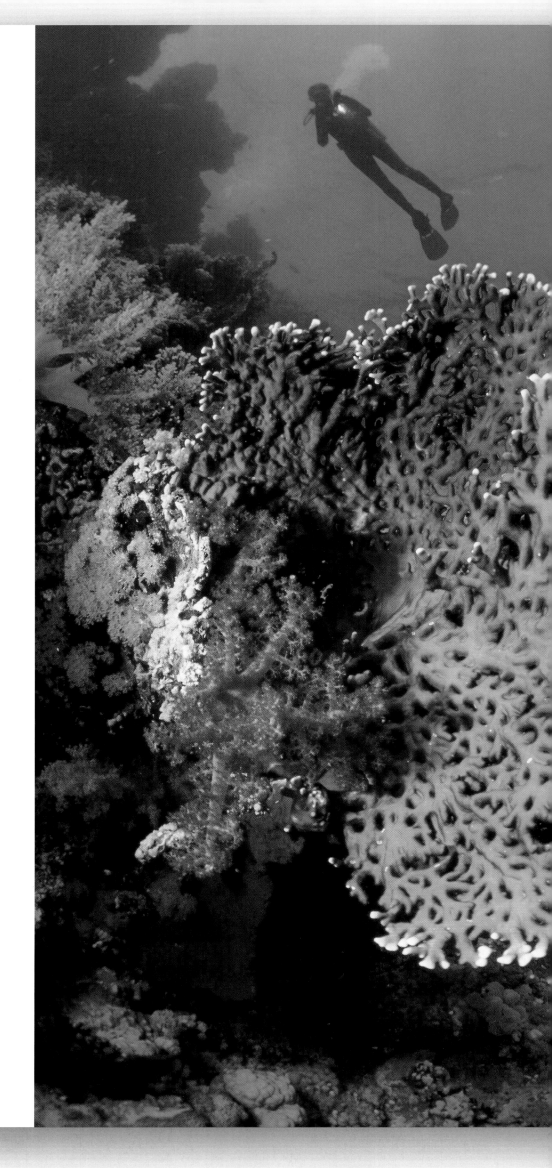

©Aladdin Books Ltd 2001

Produced by
Aladdin Books Ltd
28 Percy Street
London WIP 0LD

ISBN 0-7613-2452-6 (s&l)
ISBN 0-7613-2280-9 (pbk.)

*First published in the United States
in 2001 by*
Copper Beech Books Books,
an imprint of
The Millbrook Press
2 Old New Milford Road
Brookfield, Connecticut 06804

Project Management
SGA design & illustration agency
Hadleigh
Suffolk IP7 5AP

Project Manager
Philippa Jackaman (SGA)

Designer
Phil Kay

Editor
Linda Sonntag

Picture Researcher
Brian Hunter Smart

Illustrators
Geoff Ball
John Butler
James Field
Piers Harper
Terry Riley
Stephen Sweet

Printed in Belgium
All rights reserved

Cataloging-in-Publication data is
on file at the Library of Congress.

The author, Linda Sonntag, has
written for children on a wide
range of topics including the living
world, human biology, earth sciences,
and cultures and traditions.

The consultant, Trevor Norton,
is Professor of Marine Biology at
Liverpool University and Director
of Port Erin Marine Laboratory on
the Isle of Man. He is the author of
several books, including
Stars Beneath the Sea and
Reflections on a Summer Sea.

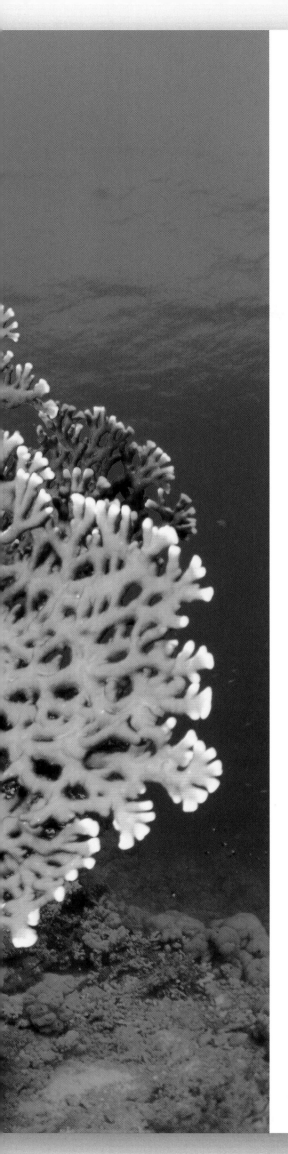

CONTENTS

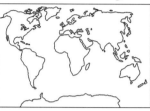

INTRODUCTION

From space our planet looks brilliant blue—water covers nearly three-quarters of its surface. The world's oceans are immense, with more than 100 billion gallons (450 billion liters) of water for every inhabitant on Earth, yet until recently they were largely unknown. Only over the past few decades have scientists discovered how ancient geological forces created the continents and oceans, shaping extraordinary underwater landscapes that include the longest mountain chains, the deepest trenches, and the vastest plains on Earth.

By studying the information new technology delivers about the oceans, scientists believe they will find the key to climate change and global warming. In the oceans we have a rich source of food, energy, and mineral resources. Yet we threaten our seas with pollution. The science of oceanography will help us understand how the oceans work and how we can become better stewards of our fragile world.

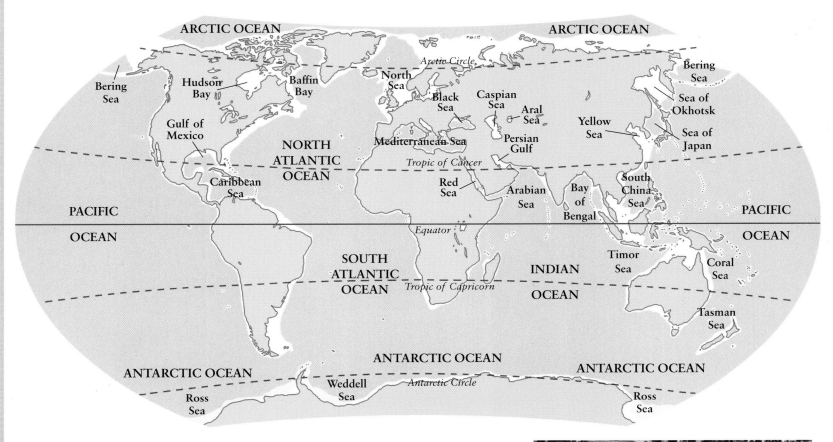

Heroes of the seas

From ancient times adventurers have crossed the seas. They sailed in quest of knowledge, or new lands and trading partners, or peoples to conquer and exploit. The voyages of some of history's great navigators are well known. Christopher Columbus is famous for crossing the Atlantic in his ships the *Niña, Pinta, and Santa Maria* (right) in 1492. But the oceans also have many unsung heroes. In modern times the Vietnamese boat people (far right) made epic voyages as they fled their homeland to take refuge in far-off Hong Kong.

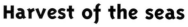

Harvest of the seas

The oceans are a rich source of food—90 percent of sea creatures provide a meal for other marine life, but humans are the biggest predators of all. How much can we take from the sea without exhausting it? Today's yearly harvest of nearly 80 million tons is five times bigger than it was half a century ago. Half that much again is wasted every year—fish thrown back dead, among them other creatures snared and killed, such as dolphins. Yet scientists believe that if the oceans' resources were properly managed, there would be enough food for all.

The web of life

Take a scoop of seawater in your cupped hands and you hold a feast of millions of microscopic animals and simple plants. Called plankton, these minute organisms form the basis of the ocean's food chain, which runs from the small shrimplike krill (inset) to the mighty baleen whale. From the mysteriously calm waters of the Sargasso Sea, to the miraculous coral reefs of the Pacific, the kelp forests of the South Atlantic, and the steaming mangrove swamps of West Africa, the world's oceans offer abundant habitats to an astonishing array of wildlife.

Into the future

People have always wanted to explore the mysterious beauty of the underwater world. The development of underwater cameras, submersibles, and robotic sensors has greatly increased our knowledge of the deep. On the right, a research station under the Red Sea studies some of the richest and least spoiled coral reefs in the world. Below right, a diver peers into a giant clam on Australia's Great Barrier Reef. Information comes also from far above the Earth, where satellites track winds and

measure the surface temperature of the ocean. It also comes from humble sources: seeds and fruits that fall into the ocean from trees in the tropics are carried thousands of miles to distant shores, revealing the paths of ocean currents. New studies help scientists to understand the finely balanced systems of our planet, and may lead them to unravel puzzles such as El Niño, the freak water current that disrupts weather patterns across the globe.

ACROSS THE OCEANS

People have always taken advantage of tides, currents, and winds to go with the flow and travel by water. The earliest craft were simple floats and rafts, but then someone hollowed out a log and invented the boat. This wooden boat was the prototype for all the ocean-going vessels of the modern age.

The first ocean crossings were made long ago. Intrepid aboriginals arrived in Australia across the waves from Southeast Asia around 60,000 B.C. A mere 3,000 years ago the greatest seafarers of the ancient world, the Polynesians, were sailing the Pacific to settle islands scattered across 8 million square miles (20 million sq km) of water. The Greeks, the Chinese, and the Vikings all ventured into unknown waters far from home. The great age of discovery began in the late 1400s when the Europeans started looking for trade routes. The Portuguese voyaged down the west coast of Africa to find a new water route to India and the spice lands of the east. Columbus sailed west looking for a different route to India and landed in the Americas. Magellan's expedition became the first to sail around the world and prove that it was round. And Captain Cook led expeditions across the Pacific to Australia.

Voyage into the past

A fascination with the feats of the ancient seafarers has led modern adventurers to recreate their voyages in replica craft. In 1947, Thor Heyerdahl sailed the raft *Kon Tiki* 4,030 miles (6,500 km) across the Pacific Ocean to demonstrate that South Americans could have colonized Polynesian islands. In 1970, he sailed from Morocco to the Caribbean in a reed boat, hoping to prove that Egyptians could have sailed to the Americas thousands of years before Columbus.

Greek merchant ship

The Greeks have always been a seafaring people—it is because the ancient Greeks cut down their trees to build warships that Greek islands are so bare today. Greek merchant ships had oars, sails, and anchors, and sailors used weighted lines to measure the depth of the seabed. By 500 B.C., Greek cities had established trading colonies in southern Italy and on the northern coast of the Black Sea. The colonies sent grain and timber in return for pottery and jewelry. The Greeks also traded in hides, salted fish, wine, and luxuries such as rich garments, fine metalwork, and perfume flasks.

Spanish Armada

In 1588, Phillip II of Spain sent his mighty Armada of 130 ships to attack England. Though the English fleet numbered 197, their ships were smaller. The Armada anchored off Calais in the English Channel, but was forced out to sea by fireships. Then the English defeated the invaders in a huge sea battle off Gravelines in France. Led by Howard of Effingham, the English battleships out-maneuvered the much heavier Spanish galleons. Sir Francis Drake (inset) was a squadron commander during the battle. He had already won recognition from Queen Elizabeth I for his voyage round the world in the *Golden Hind*.

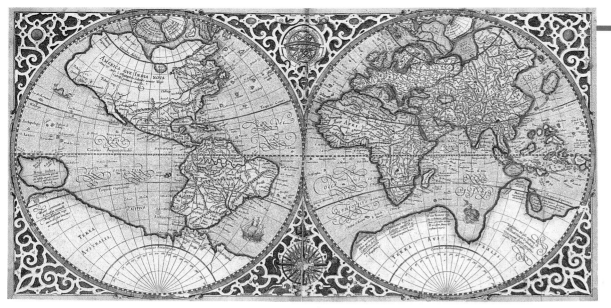

Mercator's map

Early sailors steered by the stars. By 1200, the magnetic compass was in use. A later invention was the astrolabe, which enabled navigators to calculate latitude by observing the Sun at midday. In the late 1500s, the maps of Gerardus Mercator offered a new way of looking at the world on paper. His system used lines of latitude and longitude and enabled sailors to plan more accurate routes.

Submarines

German U-boats were used to fight the Allies in both World Wars. They were driven by a diesel engine for surface travel and by battery-powered electric motors underwater. A new era of military strategy began in 1954, when the U.S. launched the first ever nuclear-powered submarine, the *Nautilus*. Propulsion in a nuclear submarine is by steam turbine driving a propeller.

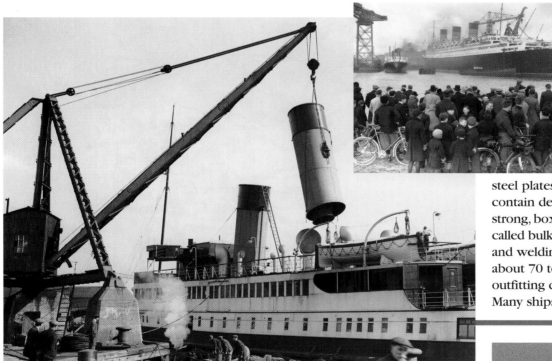

Clydeside

The shipyards on the Clyde River in Scotland built the fabled Cunard liners, including the *Queen Mary* (top left). Traditionally, shipbuilding needed the skills of hundreds of workers, such as welders, electricians, and painters. Nowadays, ships are made of steel plates and are built in sections that already contain decking and other fittings. The series of strong, boxlike sections are reinforced by walls called bulkheads. Computers often control the cutting and welding of the steel plates. When the ship is about 70 to 90 percent finished, it is towed to an outfitting dock for the final stages of construction. Many ships are now built in the Far East.

Hovercraft

British designer Christopher Cockerell invented the hovercraft in 1959. He wanted to build a craft that floated on air, not water, and made his first experiments with a coffee can and a vacuum cleaner. Large fans blowing underneath the vessel make the hovercraft's cushion of air. The hull rises 6 feet (2 m) above the water and travels forward with its propellers pushing air not water. The air under the hull is held in place by a flexible "skirt." The hovercraft is also used to travel on land.

HOW OCEANS WORK

In the beginning there was no water on Earth—it was far too hot. The mainly molten surface erupted with volcanoes that spewed forth clouds of steam. Violent lightning storms raged continuously and showers of meteorites bombarded the planet from outer space. There was no oxygen in the atmosphere—instead, storms churned up a scalding mix of hydrogen, methane, ammonia, and water vapor. These gases were too thin to act as a shield against the Sun's fierce radiation, so Earth was bathed in intense ultraviolet light.

Then about 3,800 mya (million years ago), Earth's temperature fell below the boiling point and water vapor began to condense into rain. The rain carved rivers as it flowed down the mountains, and filled low-lying areas to form primeval seas. The deluge went on for thousands of years. In these harsh conditions and inhospitable setting the first microscopic life forms emerged. As they photosynthesized (made food from sunlight), they began to produce oxygen. Increasing concentrations of oxygen in the atmosphere gradually built up the ozone layer, protecting the Earth from the Sun's harmful radiation and allowing the development of other life forms.

200 million years ago

100 million years ago

50 million years ago

present day

Continental drift

Parts of today's landmasses look as though they once fitted together. In fact, 200 mya they were all part of one supercontinent called Pangaea. The Earth's outer layer consists of continental plates that float on a hot layer of rock called the mantle. Heat from the Earth's core creates currents in the mantle, which move the plates around, pushing up mountains where they collide and changing the shapes of landmasses and oceans. This process, called continental drift, continues today. The Atlantic is slowly growing and the Pacific is shrinking. In millions of years, the map of the world will look different again.

Vital gases

The early planet, fraught with storms and volcanic eruptions, was charged with the energy that transformed itself into life. In 1952, a chemist named Henry Miller conducted a laboratory experiment to find out if he could create life by replicating the conditions on Earth 3,000 mya. He put water in a flask with methane, ammonia, and hydrogen. Then he passed an electric current through the mix to simulate lightning. The next day he discovered that amino acids were present, which form proteins—the building blocks of life.

The evidence of fossils

In 1915, a German scientist named Alfred Wegener proposed the theory of continental drift. His study of fossils had convinced him that the continents were once all joined together, but had split up and drifted apart. He pointed out that fossils of a similar type had formed at the same time on both sides of the Atlantic. Since there was no way the animals could have walked across, the landmasses must once have been joined. Wegener's theory was finally proved beyond doubt when the seabed was explored in the 1960s.

Rain

Wind

Evaporation

Seawater

Seawater is 96.5 percent water (hydrogen and oxygen combined) and 2.9 percent salt (sodium chloride). The remaining 0.6 percent consists of other elements, including calcium, magnesium, and potassium, all of which are washed off the land. Water pressure increases with depth. The tremendous pressure in the ocean depths keeps the water from freezing, though it is colder than 32°F (-1°C). Temperature and salinity (saltiness) affect water density. Cold salty water is denser, so it sinks beneath warmer surface water. The difference in density keeps the water moving to form currents.

Water cycle

Earth's water is constantly in motion. Heat from the Sun causes water to evaporate from oceans, rivers, and plants. As it rises, water vapor cools and condenses into droplets that form clouds. When clouds are swept higher, the droplets become denser until they are so heavy that they fall. Warm air rising from cumulonimbus clouds produces convectional rain. Rain falling from cool clouds over mountains is orographic rain. Rain that falls when an area of high pressure collides with an area of low pressure is frontal rain. Rain falls into rivers or seas, and drains down into groundwater, and the whole process begins again. This is called the water cycle.

THE PRIMEVAL SEA

No one knows how life began—but the leap from inorganic chemicals to primitive cells took place in the primeval oceans over four billion years ago.

In the beginning there were microscopic bacteria and protozoa. A film of algae was probably the first life form visible to the naked eye. The earliest traces of multicelled animals are imprints left by soft-bodied creatures in sandstone found in South Australia. They show that primitive jellyfish, sea pens, and worms existed around 600 mya. Early worms and arthropods were the first creatures with nerve cells joined together to make primitive brains. These sea creatures went on to develop hard parts and shells that leave fossils. The start of the fossil record, 570 mya, is called the Cambrian period. It saw a huge explosion of life forms, such as sponges. Around 510 mya the first vertebrates appeared— primitive fish with bony plates around their heads. These were placoderms, ancestors of amphibians, the first creatures to move onto land.

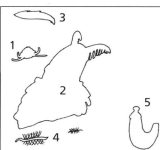

Lizards of the deep

The Jurassic period (205–145 mya) brought warm seas and abundant life forms. While dinosaurs roamed the Earth, other reptiles flourished in the seas. Like their relatives on land, they breathed air, which meant coming to the surface to fill their lungs. Their long, lithe bodies propelled them quickly through the water in pursuit of prey: fish and other animals. They may have reproduced like today's reptiles by laying eggs, dragging themselves on to land with their front legs and scraping a nest in the sand in which to bury them.

Bottom to top (heads): Hainosaurus, Tylosaurus, Plotosaurus, Platecarpus, Clidastes.

Rise and fall

The Cretaceous period (145–65 mya) saw the sea level rise higher than it had ever been, and North America became divided by a huge seaway that stretched from the Arctic to the Gulf of Mexico. A variety of marine creatures lived in this shallow body of water and left vital clues about their appearance, lifestyle, and habitat in a great band of fossils that extends down North America today. These fossils formed in sedimentary rock laid down on the seabed, and came to light millions of years later as the land rose or the sea fell. Fossils also reveal that most of Europe, excepting Scandinavia, lay under the sea at this time.

Left to right: Archelon (a gigantic turtle over 13 feet (4 m) long), Platecarpus, ammonites (ancestors of the modern nautilus), Xiphactinus, Tylosaurus, Elasmosaurus.

The Cambrian seabed

In Canada the Burgess Shale, a sedimentary rock from the Cambrian period, has preserved fossils of sea creatures that lived 570 mya. This was a time of intense evolutionary diversification, when the ancestors of most of today's animal groups probably first appeared. About 90 percent of these creatures became extinct, taking their experimental designs with them.

Anomalocaris (1 and 2) had hooked claws and powerful jaws. Pikaia (3) was a type of worm, the first with a primitive brain. Hallucigenia (4) strutted on stilts, waving its tentacles. Marrella (5) was an arthropod, the commonest creature of the Burgess Shale.

THE CHANGING SEA

HOW OCEANS WORK

Oceans change shape as Earth's continental plates push against one another. When plates collide, they push great slabs of the seabed above sea level to form mountain ranges. Fossils of seashells have been found even on Mount Everest.

Thousands of islands began as seabed volcanoes. Ascension Island, in the Atlantic Ocean, formed when molten rock pushed through Earth's crust on the underwater mountain range known as the Mid-Atlantic Ridge. In the Pacific Ocean volcanic islands form where the ocean plate plunges down into Earth's mantle. Other islands form over a hot spot, where magma deep inside the Earth burns a hole through the crust.

Fire beneath the Earth shapes the sea, and so does ice. During the ice ages, glaciers carved deep grooves into the Earth's surface, which filled with water as they melted. As the sea level rose, it created islands such as Britain, cutting them off from the continents to which they were once joined. Today, as the planet warms up and the polar icecaps melt, the seas are swelling and rising further, threatening to flood many coasts and submerge low-lying islands. Shorelines are also shaped by winds and waves, and by currents that drag deposits of sand, gravel, and boulders. People are changing the seas with pollution and dumping.

Cave

Cliff

Arch

Stack

Tides and waves

Mountains

Valley eroded by glacier

Headlands, arches, and stacks

When waves reach the shore they are slowed down in the shallows and pushed along the coast, crashing with full force against jutting headlands. The waves wear clefts (cracks) in the headlands that deepen to form caves. As air is repeatedly forced into a cave by the incoming tide, a hole may form in the cave roof. Where two caves have formed on opposite sides of a headland, the sea crashes away at them until they meet in the middle, forming an arch. The arch is made wider and wider, until the roof falls in and just a stack is left. The stack eventually crumbles into the sea. This process takes hundreds of years.

How fjords are formed

During the last ice age, huge glaciers ground their way slowly down from the polar icecaps toward the lower latitudes. Boulders and rubble trapped inside these frozen rivers wore away at the land and carved it into deep valleys. Then as the ice retreated 10,000 years ago, meltwater poured down these valleys and into the sea. The sea swelled and its level rose. Fjords are the result—narrow, steep-sided inlets found around the coasts of Norway and New Zealand's South Island.

Undersea volcano erupts to form an island

Coral grows on the solidifed mineral-rich lava

The volcano sinks beneath the sea

The coral reef remains—an atoll surrounded by a lagoon

How an atoll forms

An atoll is a circular coral reef surrounding a lagoon. An atoll develops around a volcano. First a coral reef grows on the mineral-rich lava that erupted out of the volcano. Then, as the Earth's continental plates shift and the volcano is moved away from the hot spot that caused it to erupt, its weight makes it sink. At the same time, the reef grows up toward the sunlit surface waters around it. Eventually, the volcano disappears under the sea, and the atoll remains. Atolls are often found in chains in the Pacific.

Volcanic islands

Many Pacific islands form when an undersea volcano erupts, rising above the surface of the water. The Hawaiian Islands far out in the ocean have formed in this way. Two Hawaiian volcanoes, Kilauea and Mauna Loa, erupt, throwing up plumes of fiery lava. A third volcano, Loihi, is rising under the sea and will eventually take its place in the island chain. The Hawaiian Islands are forming over a hot spot where molten rock bubbles up through Earth's crust.

How salt forms in the Dead Sea

This photo shows clumps of salt crystals in the shallows of the Dead Sea, the saltiest sea on Earth. The Dead Sea lies inland, over 1,300 feet (400 m) below sea level, between Israel and Jordan. It is fed by the River Jordan, which both countries use for irrigation. The water levels in the Dead Sea have fallen so far that the sea has divided into two. As the Sun evaporates the water, strange salt formations are left behind. The same thing happened in the Mediterranean Sea when it dried up six million years ago.

Sea pollution

This diagram illustrates some of the many causes of sea pollution. The world's oceans are often treated as a garbage dump. Refuse, sewage, toxic, and even nuclear waste are dumped into the sea without consideration for the harm this does to marine ecology and to people. Factories pump poisonous effluents into rivers, which wash them into the sea, and chemicals used by farmers are washed off the land. Oil is routinely discharged from ships to clean their tanks. The result is that toxic chemicals have been found in animals thousands of miles from the pollution source.

Agricultural chemicals

Nuclear power stations discharge radioactive water into the sea

Dredgers dump sand and gravel on the seabed

Oil spill from wrecked tanker

Sewage works

Untreated sewage is piped out to sea

Polluted clouds rain into sea

Burned chemical particles drift into sea from waste incineration

Sewage sludge is dumped at sea by barges

WAVES AND TIDES

HOW OCEANS WORK

The water of the oceans is never still. Two of its movements are tides and waves. Tides alter the spread of the ocean, and waves change its surface.

Twice a day, the sea rises and comes flooding in onto the shore, then ebbs, or goes back out again. These changes in sea level are high tide and low tide. They are caused mainly by the pull of the Moon and the Sun. The Moon's pull on the Earth's oceans is more than twice as strong as the Sun's. It draws the waters into a bulge on the side of the Earth that it faces. To balance this effect, the Earth's rotation makes the waters on the opposite side of the Earth bulge up as well. The height and pace of tides are affected by weather and geography—the slope of the beach, the shape of the coast, and the size of the ocean basin.

Waves are formed by winds rippling the ocean's surface to form ridges and valleys. Winds blowing steadily over open seas can create a huge swell, with wavelengths (the length between one crest and the next) of more than half a mile (1 km). A hurricane can raise towering waves at least 50 feet (15 m) high (from crest to trough).

Wave breaks on the shore

Wave peaks

Wind direction

Water circulates while the wave moves on—like a rope being shaken

Winds make waves

A breeze out at sea blows up gentle waves. If the wind is stronger, the wave crests steepen. Stronger still, and heaving waves topple into a foaming spray. But though the wave moves forward, the water it is made of hardly moves at all. Instead, it follows a circular pattern. When waves arrive at a shallow beach, they surge smoothly up the shore. On a steep shore, they rear up and crash down as plunging breakers. The further the waves have rolled, the higher they are.

The Moon and tides

The way sunlight falls on the Earth and the Moon (right) shows that they are in line with the Sun. The combined pull of the Moon and the Sun results in a specially high tide called a spring tide. Spring tides have the greatest range between high and low tides, and happen at new Moon (when the Moon is between Earth and Sun, as here) and full Moon (when Earth is in the middle). At the first and third quarter of the Moon, the Moon and Sun pull at right angles to the Earth, causing a neap tide. Neap tides have the lowest range between high and low tides.

High and low tides

In seas that are almost completely surrounded by land, such as the Red Sea, there is hardly any difference between high and low tide. On coasts open to the ocean, the tidal range is usually 3 to 16 feet (2 to 5 m). But in wide, shallow bays and estuaries, the tide comes racing in across the flats, then recedes just as fast. At high tide the Bay of Fundy in eastern Canada, is full of water, but at low tide it is nearly empty. It has a tidal range of 43 feet (13 m), one of the greatest in the world.

Tidal power

Ocean power is a source of energy that doesn't pollute and won't run out—unlike fossil fuels. This tidal power station on the Rance estuary in France was the first to harness ocean power. The dam is built across the estuary. The turbines, situated below the waterline, are turned to produce electricity as the tide ebbs and flows. So far, such systems have proved more expensive than burning fossil fuels—the search is still on for renewable alternatives. Some ideas might be to harness wave power, or the Sun's energy, stored as heat in the sea.

2. Ocean thermal energy conversion (OTEC) harnesses temperature differences in the water

1. Flexible air bags harness wave power

3. Salter's Duck harnesses wave power

Direction of waves

Warm surface water

Cold water drawn up from the depths

Air in

Air out

Harnessing ocean power

This diagram shows three alternatives being developed to harness ocean power out at sea. 1 Tidal power compresses air in flexible bags, which drives gas turbine generators. 2 Ocean Thermal Energy Conversion (OTEC) uses the big difference in temperature between warm surface waters and cold deep waters to condense and evaporate ammonia. As the ammonia passes through the condensation cycle, it drives turbines that generate electricity. 3 Salter's Duck is one of several designs that involve huge rockers. Rolling waves force water through valves to drive turbines. This system depends on a constant supply of high waves.

15

STORMS AT SEA

HOW OCEANS WORK

Ocean storms are violent movements of air and water. They create some of the planet's most spectacular and destructive weather events.

Air becomes wind when differences in temperature and pressure around the globe cause it to move. The heat of the Sun powers the winds, which drive the waves and the surface currents of the oceans. Strong winds become powerful storms. Across the Atlantic Ocean, winter gales build up huge rollers that batter the western coasts of France and Spain. Summer storms are common in the tropics. Here, warm damp air rises, then condenses, falling as torrential rain. Huge amounts of heat energy are released as lightning. As the warm air rises, the Earth's spin throws it into a spiral. Cold air is sucked in below, and enters the cycle of heating, rising and spinning. The result is a vast system of whirling clouds called a hurricane.

As it travels across the sea, a hurricane builds up speed, enabling it to hit islands and coastal areas with tremendous destructive force. Hurricanes fade and die as they move across land or cooler water. Tsunami are powerful waves that can travel thousands of miles at high speed, crashing down on coasts with devastating force. Spectacular waterspouts are phenomena that rarely cause damage.

Devastation

A scene of devastation in Darwin, Australia, after Cyclone Tracey hit in 1974. Hurricanes are monitored by satellite so that people in their path can be warned and evacuated. Sometimes aircraft try to divert a hurricane from hitting the coast. They fly into the large calm eye of the storm from above and "seed" the clouds with salt or iodine in an attempt to make another eye, which will take the hurricane off in a different direction.

A hurricane is born

Hurricane Dennis develops in the Caribbean in 1999. Thunderclouds gather (1) and begin to swirl (2). In five days the hurricane has fully formed (3). It can be up to 300 miles (480 km) wide with winds up to 105 mph (250 km/h). At the center is the eye, an area of calm amid whirling cloud. "Hurricane" means evil spirit in the Caribbean. Hurricanes are called cyclones in the Indian Ocean and typhoons in the Pacific. Each storm is given a name in an alphabetical list.

The world's winds

At the equator, air warmed by the Sun gets lighter and rises, creating an area of low pressure in its wake. At the poles, cold, dense air sinks, creating an area of high pressure. Air is drawn from high-pressure areas to low-pressure areas, which is what makes the wind blow. The direction of winds is also affected by the Earth's rotation. It causes them to veer to the right of their direction of travel in the northern hemisphere, and to the left of their direction of travel in the southern hemisphere. All weather systems and ocean currents are pulled by the Earth's rotation in the same way. This is called the Coriolis effect, and can even be observed as the bathwater goes down the drain—clockwise in the northern hemisphere, and counterclockwise in the southern hemisphere.

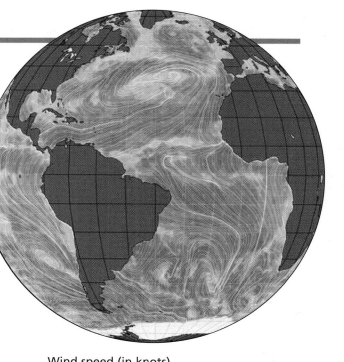

Wind speed (in knots)

| 50 | 40 | 30 | 20 | 10 | 00 |

Tsunami

An underwater earthquake or volcano sets off a series of huge waves called tsunami. Traveling across the ocean, they can reach 125 miles (200 km) in length, and speeds of 435 mph (700 km/h). At only 20 inches (0.5 m) high, they are hardly noticeable to ships, but when they reach land, the shelving seabed causes them to slow down, rear up, and crash-land from crests nearly 100 feet (30 m) high. One tsunami created waves more than 1,700 feet (518 m) high!

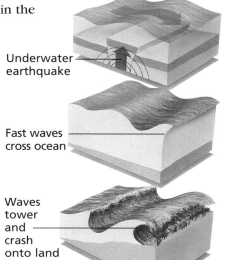

Underwater earthquake

Fast waves cross ocean

Waves tower and crash onto land

Tropical storm

Huge cumulus or cumulonimbus clouds form in the tropics as warm damp air rises, causing violent electric storms to light up the night sky. In late summer when the sea is at its warmest, hundreds of storms come together and rotate in a great low pressure system that forms a hurricane.

Waterspout

When a tornado forms over water, it creates a waterspout. They are most common in the tropics. A spinning funnel of air dips down from a huge cloud to touch the sea, and sucks up a pillar of foaming water that can be 1,000 feet (300 m) wide and 3,000 feet (900 m) tall. Sailors once believed water-spouts to be sea monsters. Waterspouts rarely cause any damage. They travel at less than 30 mph (50 km/h) and last only 15 minutes. Tornadoes cause much greater devastation when over land.

OCEAN CURRENTS

Currents flow through the world's oceans like mighty rivers, driven by the Sun and winds. The Earth's rotation twists them to the right, or clockwise, in the northern hemisphere, and to the left, or counterclockwise, in the southern hemisphere. On the surface of the oceans, currents travel in huge loops called gyres (from the Greek *gyros*, meaning circle).

Water currents in the depths have a different journey. In the polar regions of the Atlantic, water is cooled by ice, and sinks, displacing the warmer water below. As it flows south, the strong cold current is joined by dense salty water flowing out of the Mediterranean Sea. It travels on, crossing the tropics at great depths, pushing through the South Atlantic, and eventually spreading around the Antarctic. Moving north, it mixes with warmer water in the Indian and Pacific Oceans. It reenters the Atlantic, rising and flowing back northward along the surface all the way to Greenland and the Labrador Sea, where it chills and becomes cold heavy water once more. The cycle then starts all over again. This trip can take many years to complete.

Surface currents

Surface currents may be as warm as 86°F (30°C) or as cold as 28°F (-2°C). They have an important effect on the world's climates and weather. In the Atlantic, the Gulf Stream brings warm water from the Gulf of Mexico and the Caribbean sweeping up the coast of North America and Newfoundland, then past the British Isles. With global warming melting polar ice, the Gulf Stream could be weakened and deflected from its course, causing the climate in the parts of the world that it warms today—such as Britain—to grow much colder.

- ■ warm currents
- ■ cold currents

Glove overboard!

Seeds and fruits can drift thousands of miles on ocean currents. Dropping from trees in the tropics, they are washed into the sea and may journey for as long as 30 years before landing on a beach far from their origins. This hockey glove was one of 34,000 items lost overboard from a container ship during a Pacific storm in 1994. About 500 gloves and sneakers have been washed up on beaches in the U.S., Canada, and Alaska. With the aid of computers, scientists are plotting their probable journey across the ocean, discovering more about how currents work.

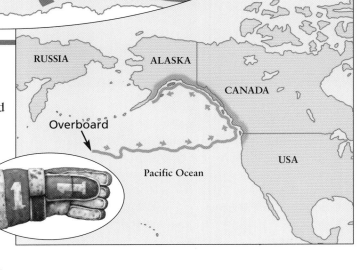

RUSSIA   ALASKA

CANADA

Overboard

USA

Pacific Ocean

Deep water currents

Oceanographers hope their study of deep water currents will help them understand climate change and discover clues to the origins of El Niño and other weather phenomena. They use a CTD (conductivity-temperature-depth) recorder to measure the temperature and salinity (saltiness) of water at different depths. The research ship visits precise locations determined by global positioning satellites. The CTD instrument with its sample bottles is lowered over the side and takes 40 samples per second down to depths of 8,200 feet (2,500 m). Results are plotted on a chart and reveal how, where, and when currents move.

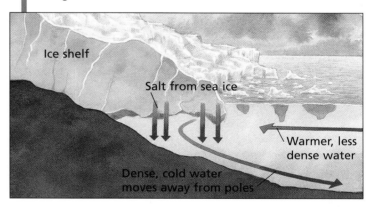

cold currents

El Niño

Changes to an ocean current can have a devastating impact on climate. About every four years a huge body of hot water gathers in the Pacific off Ecuador and Peru. Fish catches decline as fish head for colder waters, and rain falls on deserts. The ocean heats up near Christmas, so fishermen call it El Niño (the boy) after the Christ child. These satellite pictures show the warm water, in white, massing in 1997. Sometimes El Niño is followed by a cold current called La Niña (the girl). For reasons not yet understood, La Niña reverses the effects of El Niño, causing drought where there was flooding, and flooding where there was drought.

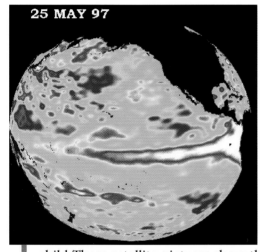

25 MAY 97

A cold current is born

Deep in the ocean, currents carry dense cold water from the Greenland icecap in the Arctic through the Atlantic to the tropics and beyond. These deep water currents are driven by differences in the density of sea water. Water melting under the Greenland icecap is very cold, and heavy with salt. Cold salty water is dense and sinks, displacing water that is less dense, so setting a current in motion. It moves slowly, spreading toward the equator at the rate of a few yards a day. Deep water flow is called thermohaline circulation.

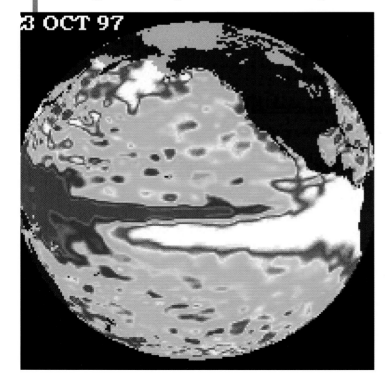

3 OCT 97

Ice shelf

Salt from sea ice

Warmer, less dense water

Dense, cold water moves away from poles

Climate in upheaval

This seal has starved to death, a victim of El Niño off California. The fish that seals feed on swam deep in search of cooler waters, where the seals could not reach them. In 1997-8 El Niño disrupted the world's climate in ways not yet understood, claiming the lives of about 2,000 people around the globe. Forest fires raged in Brazil and Sumatra, Florida suffered severe drought, there were floods in Kenya and Sudan, and mud slides developed in Peru, where a stretch of desert became a lake. With the aid of modern technology, scientists hope to be able to predict El Niño, so that lives can be saved and farmers can plan ahead.

19

UNDER THE OCEAN

Under the ocean lies a dramatic landscape. It is only since the 1960s that submersibles, using sonar and magnetometers, have begun to explore its mysteries. They discovered that the seabed has vast sweeping plains, active volcanoes, plunging trenches, and the longest continuous mountain ranges on the planet.

The land dips into the sea at the continental shelf, a broad rim about 600 feet (180 m) deep. The continental slope plunges steeply to a depth of 10,000 feet (3,000 m). Stretching across the ocean floor is the abyssal plain. Further out, ridges of underwater hills and then mountains rise up 6,500 to 13,000 feet (2,000 – 4,000 m) high, spreading from a central rift, or crack, in Earth's crust. The deepest places in the ocean are trenches formed when one plate on the Earth's crust dives beneath another. The highest places are mountains and volcanoes that rise out of the ocean to form islands.

The ocean floor

Researching the geography of the ocean floor has given scientists important clues about how our planet was formed—and goes on changing. The hot rock welling up at the ocean ridge pushes the plates that form the Earth's crust further apart. The plate that is shunted away collides with the next plate—it either buckles up against it to form a mountain range, or dives underneath it, back into the molten heart of the planet, creating a massively deep trench. The neighboring plate is lifted up, sometimes so far that its highest points rise above the surface of the sea, forming an island arc.

Ocean trench

Volcanic islands forming an island arc

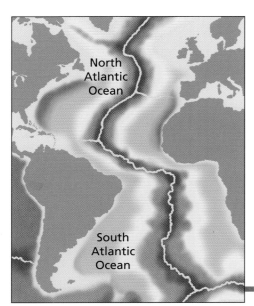

0   million years   180

Mid-Atlantic Ridge

A ridge in the ocean floor is the crack that divides two plates of the Earth's crust. Hot magma, which is molten rock from deep inside the Earth, wells up through the crack, then cools to make a new ocean floor. The crack of young rock at the Mid-Atlantic Ridge runs the entire length of the Atlantic Ocean. It is easy to see from this magnetic map how the ridge is the "seam" where the continents were once joined together.

North Atlantic Ocean

South Atlantic Ocean

Sediments wash off the land

Continental shelf

Seamount
(underwater
volcano)

Ocean ridge

Continental slope

Molten rock rises
under ocean ridge

Plates
pulling
apart

Abyssal plain

One plate dives
beneath the next

What lives where?

Creatures live at all depths in the ocean, but plants grow only in the sunlit zone, where there is light. Some drift in the water, others are anchored to the seabed. Birds snatch fish from shoals darting just below the waves, and sea mammals surface to breathe. Mammals also dive further down to feed on fish in the twilight zone, where little light penetrates and the waters are very cold. The strange creatures that live in the deepest waters are specially adapted to withstand tremendous water pressure, cold, and inky darkness. The seabed has different zones too—from the shallows of the continental shelf to the depths of the abyssal plain—each providing a habitat for a huge range of life forms.

THE SUNLIGHT ZONE

The sunlit surface waters are a living soup of tiny floating organisms called plankton. Phytoplankton (very small plants) and zooplankton (microscopic animals) form the basis of the ocean's food chain.

Plankton need sunlight and fertile waters in which to grow. Nutrients in the sea come from minerals found on the seabed, and the remains of dead animals and droppings that fall through the water to settle there. So plankton thrive especially in areas of upwelling—where currents of cold water carrying these nutrients rise to the surface. Plankton are also plentiful along the continental shelves. In these shallower waters, debris from the seabed is churned up by storms and tides, and by rivers flowing into the sea. Where there are plankton, there will be fish feeding on them, so coastal waters are very important for the fishing industry.

Phytoplankton also have an important part to play in regulating the world's climate. In the process of photosynthesis, by which all plants make their food, they use vast amounts of carbon dioxide, one of the gases most responsible for global warming.

Phytoplankton

This map shows the distribution of phytoplankton in spring, when it is most plentiful. The red areas are the richest, followed by yellow, green, blue, and then purple. Phytoplankton are eaten by small fish and shrimps, as well as the larvae (young) of larger creatures. These animals are eaten by bigger animals still, all the way up the ocean's food chain to the largest sharks and whales.

Krill

Krill are crustaceans which are about $1/2$ to 5 inches (1 to 15 cm) in length. Inhabitants of cool seas, they feed on plankton and are eaten by whales, seals, seabirds, fish, and squid. They are also harvested by people. Krill swim in swarms of millions that are often a few miles long. Though they are small, in terms of biomass (overall weight), they are probably the most dominant species on the planet.

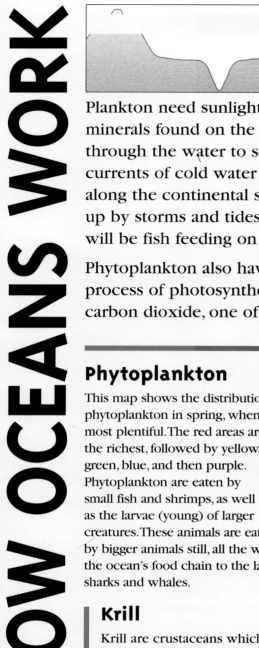

Sea otter

The sea otter rarely comes ashore, except in very stormy weather or to give birth to its pups. To rest or sleep, it wraps itself in kelp floating on the surface of the water. It dives to the seabed to fetch sea urchins, clams, and crabs. Then it lies on its back among the kelp and cracks them open by pounding them against a stone, also brought from the seabed, which it rests on its stomach. It is one of the few animals, apart from humans, that has learned how to use a tool.

Anchovies

Anchovies are members of the herring family that grow up to 8 inches (20 cm) long. Schools of thousands of anchovies swim close to the surface, feeding on plankton. Their darting silvery bodies help to camouflage them in the bright water against their predators—larger fish and diving seabirds such as pelicans. Anchovies lay their eggs close to the seabed. They hatch into larvae only 1/5 inch (5 mm) long, then drift among the plankton until they grow large enough to form schools of their own.

Baleen whale

Hanging from the right whale's upper jaw are fringed plates of a bristly material called baleen. When the whale opens its mouth to feed, water full of krill flows inside. The whale forces the water back out through the baleen, and swallows the krill left behind. One whale may eat four million krill in a day. There are several baleen whales, including the right, the blue, the fin, and the humpback. All have been brought close to extinction by the whaling industry.

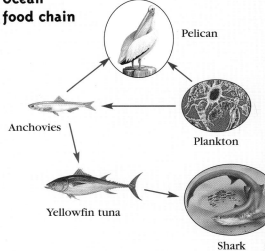

Ocean food chain

Pelican

Anchovies

Plankton

Yellowfin tuna

Shark

Kelp plants and sea urchins

Kelp can grow up to 2 feet (60 cm) a day, rivalling bamboo as the world's fastest growing plant. Rootlike structures called holdfasts anchor the plant to the seabed. Its stems and blades (leaves) stretch towards the Sun, then spread out on the surface of the water. Storms may uproot the plant, but kelp's worst enemy is the sea urchin. If these spiny creatures invade a kelp forest, they eat only the base of the plant, leaving the rest to float away and die. Many creatures that live and feed in the kelp forests would not survive without sea otters to eat the sea urchins.

23

THE TWILIGHT ZONE

HOW OCEANS WORK

From a depth of 660 feet (50 m), the waters get steadily darker and colder. This is the twilight zone, 660 to 3,300 feet (50 to 1,000 m), which gives way to the dark zone. Here, no light penetrates at all.

In the twilight zone there is not enough light for plants to grow, but a steady rain of debris drifts down from above—the remains of dead creatures and their droppings—to provide food for zooplankton, prawns, and fish, which in turn are eaten by larger fish and cruising sharks. Many animals spend their days lurking in the safety of the twilight zone, then rise to the richer waters of the surface to feed at night. The creatures of the twilight zone have adapted to the lack of light in several ways. Some produce their own light, in luminescent organs. Many have large bulging eyes for maximum vision, or eyes that point upward so they can spot their prey against the dim light from above. Some detect their prey by scent or electrical pulses. Others have evolved flat shapes, and lie camouflaged on the seabed in wait for prey.

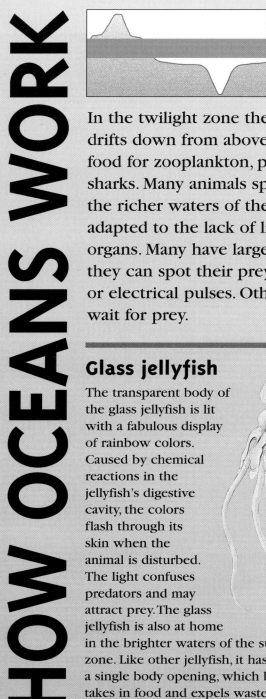

Glass jellyfish

The transparent body of the glass jellyfish is lit with a fabulous display of rainbow colors. Caused by chemical reactions in the jellyfish's digestive cavity, the colors flash through its skin when the animal is disturbed. The light confuses predators and may attract prey. The glass jellyfish is also at home in the brighter waters of the sunlit zone. Like other jellyfish, it has a single body opening, which both takes in food and expels waste. The opening is surrounded by stinging tentacles used for stunning larger prey. Jellyfish pulse gently as they drift with the current, wasting little energy in swimming.

Scarlet prawn

Deep red prawns would stand out too well in the sunlit zone and become easy prey for other creatures, but in the dim waters of the twilight zone, red appears black, so they are well camouflaged. Below the twilight zone prawns are almost transparent, hidden from their predators by the inky darkness. Small relations of the lobster, prawns swim along by rowing with their five pairs of swimmerets, paddle-shaped limbs beneath the abdomen. They feed on anything they can find, including zooplankton and dead animals.

Viperfish

A member of the bristlemouth group, the viperfish has needle-shaped lower teeth that are too long to fit inside its mouth. It uses them to trap prey that it lures inside its mouth with a glowing "fishing rod"—an extended ray or spine that has developed from the dorsal fin (the fin on its back), that dangles forward in front of its mouth with a light organ on the end. Viperfish grow to around 12 inches (30 cm) long and feed largely on hatchetfish, which are around 3 inches (8 cm long).

Hammerhead shark

This shark has its eyes and nostrils positioned at either side of the "hammer." It feeds mainly on stingrays, and the hammer may protect it from the rays' poisonous spines. It also acts as a fin, giving the shark powerful uplift at the front. Hammerheads hunt alone at night, but swim together in groups during the day. Some sharks lay eggs in leathery shells. The hammerhead's young grow in shell-less eggs inside the mother's body. When their yolk is all eaten up, they feed on the mother's blood until they are born, fully formed.

Hatchetfish

The narrow silvery body of this fish looks like the blade of an axe or hatchet, hence its name. The hatchetfish has bulging eyes that help it spot prey in the dark, and luminous patches in its mouth, which attract small creatures to swim inside. A row of light organs on its belly and under the tail confuses enemies, camouflaging the fish against the brighter water above. The pattern of light patches also helps hatchetfish to recognize members of their own species at mating time.

Stingray

The whiplike tail of the stingray is armed with a backward-pointing poisonous spine. This weapon—which can kill a human—is used only in defense against a predator such as the hammerhead shark. The ray "flies" through the water like a bird, waving its flaplike fins and gliding above the seabed in search of prey. Tiny pits in its head sense electric pulses from the muscles of shellfish and worms buried in the sand. The ray digs them out with its flattened snout and crunches them up with its teeth.

Giant squid

The giant squid is a fast-moving jet-propelled animal of the deep sea. It moves by sucking water into its torpedo-shaped mantle cavity (body sheath), then squirting it out through a siphon, which shoots the squid along backward. It has excellent vision for hunting, and it can grasp large fish with the hooks and adhesive suckers on its tentacles. Some squid have a light organ in their bodies, which they can even direct like a torch. A giant squid is the world's largest invertebrate, and can reach 56 feet (17 m) from the tip of its tentacles to its head.

25

THE INKY DEPTHS

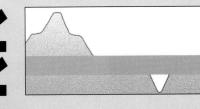

Below the twilight zone there is no light, the water is bitterly cold, and the pressure is colossal—up to 300 times greater than at the surface. There is little food because plants cannot live without light, so deep-sea creatures eat what they can get, including scraps of dead fish and droppings that sink from above.

The strange-looking animals of the ocean depths are specially adapted to the cold, the dark, and the scarcity of food. Many have a natural antifreeze in their bodies. They often have large, gaping mouths with bristling teeth to help them catch what little prey there is, and some have expanding stomachs that can receive fish even larger than themselves. Dark coloring gives camouflage, while some creatures are almost transparent. Vision is minimal in the inky blackness. Some animals have large eyes that pick up faint gleams of light, or eyes on tubes like binoculars. Others have tiny blind eyes, or no eyes at all. As many as 1,000 kinds of fish make their own light in the deep oceans. Some have luminous bacteria living under their skin. Others have special light-producing organs called photophores, or they can cause a chemical reaction that gives off light.

Deep-sea dragon

Rows of photophores (luminescent patches) are arranged along the head of the deep-sea dragon and down either side of its body. The male has more powerful lighting than his mate. Hanging beneath the creature's lower jaw is an extremely long threadlike barbel, which is highly sensitive to touch. The deep-sea dragon uses its photophores and barbel to detect the presence of prey. The photophores may also confuse and frighten predators. Deep-sea dragons grow to a length of about 12 inches (30 cm).

Gulper eel

Deep-sea fish must take advantage of any chance they can get to eat, even if their prey is larger than they are. The gulper eel hides in a rocky crevice or lies in wait on the seabed for a victim to approach, then darts forward to attack. Its huge head and gaping jaws are out of proportion to the rest of its body, and it has a large expanding stomach that can accommodate any passing victim. Another deep-sea fish, aptly called the great swallower, can partly dislocate its jaw to allow it to swallow bigger prey.

Squid

Squid are very versatile creatures found at most levels in the ocean. Their large brains and quick reactions make them extremely successful hunters. They use their tentacles to seize prey such as fish, mollusks, and crabs. A toothed tongue called a radula draws food into the mouth, where the squid crunches it with its beak. Squid are fast movers, and can reach speeds of up to 22 mph (35 km/h). During mating the male uses one of his tentacles to take a parcel of sperm from his mantle cavity and place it inside the female's mantle. She lays her eggs on the seabed.

Adapting to the deep

The stomach of the viperfish (1) is extremely elastic so that it can eat whenever food presents itself. The lanternfish (2) is named for the bright patch of luminescence on top of its head, which lights its way in the darkness. This is one of the few creatures of the deep that swims to shallower waters to feed every night. Finding a mate in the dark is difficult. The large female anglerfish (3) solves the problem by mating for life with several dwarf males. They attach themselves to her belly, and she controls their sexual function through her hormones. The Photostomias (4) is one of many fish that has light organs along its sides to help it see. The problems of exploring the deep mean that there is much more to learn about these strange fish.

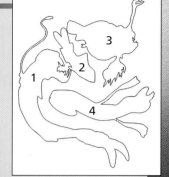

Giant oarfish

The giant oarfish lives in the Atlantic, Pacific, and Indian Oceans, swimming through the depths with a powerful whipping action of its snakelike body. It is named for its two slender, red, oarlike pelvic fins. The giant oarfish uses these to help it sense the movements of prey in the water. Its red dorsal fin peaks above the head in a magnificent crown of spines, which are usually lost with age. This creature, once the subject of terrifying legends, can grow to a staggering 30 feet (9 m) long and weigh up to 600 pounds (270 kg). Like other deep-sea fish, the oarfish has no special mechanism to help it withstand water pressure, but would not survive outside the depths where it is used to living.

Coelacanth

This huge creature is the last survivor of a group of fish that swam in the oceans 300 mya. Until recently, it was known to us only from fossils, and was thought to have died out with the dinosaurs 65 mya. But in 1938, a living coelacanth was dredged up in a trawler's net off South Africa. Since then scientists have studied these strange fish in their deep-water habitat of the western Indian Ocean. The coelacanth has a mottled blue scaly body and uses its bulbous pectoral fins to perch and rest on the seabed. The legs of the first animals to crawl on to land may have evolved from fins like these.

THE SEABED

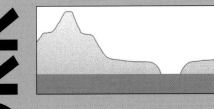

HOW OCEANS WORK

The deep seabed was explored for the first time in 1977 when the U.S. submersible *Alvin* dived 8,000 feet (2,500 m) in the Pacific. Near a spreading ridge on the seabed it found 33-feet (10-m)-tall rocky chimneys called smokers gushing scalding black water.

As the continental plates of the seabed pull apart and create a vent (opening), molten rock heats the water and sends it pluming upward, dark with dissolved minerals that settle and harden into chimneys of lava. The water that spews out of these black smokers is rich in sulfides, which are poisonous to most animals, and the temperature is hot enough to cook in. Yet large communities of deep-sea creatures gather here. This extraordinary discovery showed that not all life on this planet is directly dependent on the Sun. The sulfur-rich water feeds bacteria, which in turn nourish giant clams, tube worms, and translucent crabs. The seabed is covered with deep mud, made of plant compost and the skeletons and droppings of tiny sea animals. Some creatures guzzle the ooze to extract nourishment. Bottom-walkers have long legs to stop them sinking in, and creatures such as glass sponges have their feeding parts on tall stems, to keep them above the mud.

Alvinellid

Communities of alvinellids live in tubes on the sides of black smokers, in water hot enough to cook other creatures. They are sometimes found half in superheated water and half in the surrounding cold water—showing that they can tolerate two extremes of temperature at once.

Sea lily

Sea lilies, or crinoids, grow on the seabed, anchored by a long flexible stem. The "flowerheads" of this creature are arms that move with the ocean currents. Feathery feeding structures at their tips trap small particles of food that drift by, then the arms pass the food into the animal's upward-pointing mouth. Fossils show that sea lilies were once abundant in the oceans, though they are quite rare today, except in the deep.

Mining the deep seabed

As mines on land begin to run out of minerals, some mining companies are turning their attention to the seabed. Nodules of valuable manganese are scattered on parts of the ocean floor, but as a result of their inaccessibility, they are too expensive to retrieve. Here, a dredge on a specially designed ski-type frame is pulled across the sea floor and metals are vacuumed up a hose.

Tripod fish

Many bottom-dwellers are specially adapted to stop them from sinking into the muddy ooze of the seabed. The two pectoral fins and the tail fin of the tripod fish have long, stiff spines. Together they form a tripod, which the fish can use to help it move across the seabed, or to rest above the mud. Conserving energy, the fish remains motionless, waiting to detect food particles drifting on the current using its strong sense of smell.

Rat-tail fish

Eyes are of little use in the deep black waters, and many creatures have developed long organs like whips or whiskers that are sensitive to the vibrations of nearby prey or predators. The rat-tail fish, which grows to over 3 feet (1 m) in length, uses its fleshy, beardlike barbels to detect its food. It has to compete with ghostly pale crabs, eel-like hagfish, and red-tipped tube worms for the minute scraps and droppings that sink down to feed them through thousands of feet of water.

Sea spider

Deep-water sea spiders walk across the seabed on four pairs of long, spindly legs and swim by repeatedly jumping up and drifting down again. Sea spiders feed by sucking the juices of soft-bodied invertebrates.

Tube worms

To protect themselves against predators, many seabed dwellers, such as crabs and clams, have armored bodies. Tube worms shelter inside leathery tubes. The bright red color in the tips of the worms comes from a substance that takes in oxygen from the water, through the skin into the worm's body. Tube worms can grow up to 10 feet (3 m) long, and have light receptor cells inside their tubes. Each cell receives light from only one direction, so the cells function together as a compound eye.

29

EARLY EXPLORATION

HOW OCEANS WORK

Most early seafarers stayed within sight of land. Those who dared to cross the oceans used the stars to guide them, as well as their knowledge of winds and currents, and the routes of migrating birds.

The compass was first used in China and Arabia around 1000 A.D. Its floating magnetized needle always points in the same direction, so its potential for guiding long-distance voyagers literally changed the world. Armed with the compass, European mariners set sail in the 1400s in improved ships called caravels. Later, they mapped the western coast of Africa, sailed around Africa to India, crossed the Atlantic to the Americas, and sailed the Pacific to Australia. During the 1500s the Spanish began to explore the fascinating world under the sea. The first diving bells were shaped like big upside-down beakers with a supply of air trapped inside. Modern oceanography—the scientific study of the oceans—began in the 1800s with the pioneering expeditions of HMS *Challenger*. During a round-the-world voyage, scientists on board scoured the oceans for marine life, minerals, and clues to climate phenomena, opening up a new era of knowledge and discovery.

Astrolabe

An Arab invention from the 3rd century B.C., the astrolabe was an instrument used by astronomers. It was a flat disk showing a circular map of the heavens combined with a sighting rod that could be pivoted to point at the Sun or at bright stars. From the altitude of the Sun or a star above the horizon, astronomers could estimate local time. In the 1400s, European seafarers took the star map off the astrolabe and adapted the instrument for use in navigating. They used the new mariners' astrolabe to calculate latitude by observing the Sun at midday.

Horizon glass

Filters

Scale

Micrometer for fine adjustments

View finder

Index mirror

Sextant

Navigators used a sextant to determine latitude. A ship's navigator would line up the horizon through the middle of the viewfinder, making adjustments until the index mirror was aligned with a known star in the horizon glass. Using the angle of the star in relation to the horizon and a set of tables together with the chronometer, the navigator was able to work out his exact position. The mirror sextant was developed by the Englishman John Hadley in the mid 1700s. It was an improvement on an earlier instrument, the octant, which was accurate only when the Moon was in certain parts of the sky.

Lines of longitude cut the globe like segments of an orange

Chronometer

To calculate longitude and work out how far east or west they had traveled, mariners observed when the Sun was directly overhead, then compared this to the time of noon in their home port. An accurate clock was essential for these calculations, and in 1714 the English Board of Longitude offered a prize to anyone who could make one. The first chronometer to keep accurate time through all conditions of temperature and pressure was made by Englishman John Harrison in 1761. Over several years of testing it proved to work perfectly, even on a storm-tossed ship.

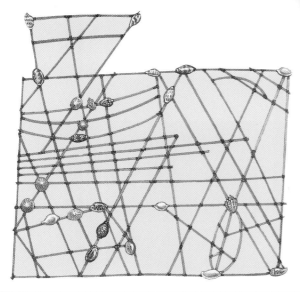

Micronesian stick map

The seafarers who settled on the Micronesian Islands in the Pacific around 5,000 years ago sailed thousands of miles across the ocean from southern China. They had no instruments to help them navigate, but studied the stars and the habits of migrating birds flying overhead. They built up a fairly good knowledge of the ocean and its weather patterns, which they shared with each other by making beautiful and intricate stick maps. In this example, the curved sticks represent ocean swells and the seashells stand for islands.

HMS *Challenger*

During their epic voyage in 1872-6 the scientists aboard HMS *Challenger* carried out an unprecedented number of experiments. They used bottles to take samples of seawater, sounding leads to measure the depth of the ocean, dredges to discover what lay on the seabed, and deep-sea thermometers to take water temperature. The naturalists on board kept detailed journals of all they saw, including bleak penguin rookeries in the Antarctic, East Indian coral and spice islands, and hostile tribes in New Guinea.

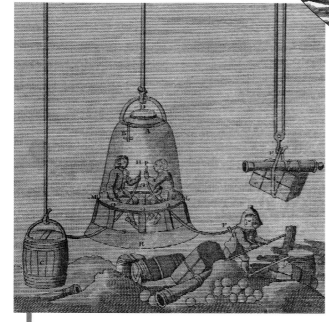

Early diving bell

In 1690, a new diving bell was invented by Englishman Edmund Halley. Big enough to hold several divers, it was open at the bottom and was lowered full of air to the seabed, where it was anchored with weights. Supplies of air were sent down in lead-lined wooden barrels and fed into the diving bell through a leather pipe. Divers took turns to explore the seabed. They walked along on the bottom wearing their ordinary clothes and a leather helmet that looked like an upside-down mixing bowl.

The "Turtle"

The *Turtle* was an early experiment in submarine warfare. This wooden vessel held a one-man crew and was designed to deliver a delayed-action mine to an enemy ship. It was used in 1776 during the Revolutionary War in an attempt to blow up an English ship blockading New York Harbor. The operator moved the Turtle by means of pedals that he worked with his hands and feet. His head stuck up into a raised helmet with portholes on top of the vessel, and he breathed air that he renewed and expelled with a pump. A buildup of carbon dioxide inside the vessel made the operator feel light-headed and the mine missed its target. Amazingly, both the ship and the operator survived.

NEW FRONTIERS

HOW OCEANS WORK

The changes in global climate and the depletion of Earth's land resources are lending a new urgency to the study of the oceans. Today oceanography is helping scientists predict the future of our planet.

From high above the Earth, satellites monitor weather patterns and ocean currents.On the oceans, floating sensors send back a constant stream of data for analysis. They will soon be accompanied by a fleet of submarine research robots looking for clues to climate change. The contours of the seabed are mapped with a bathyscan. Its echo-sounding system scans the ocean floor with a beam of acoustic pulses. Research ships use deep-sea drilling to bring up samples of rock, while dredges and grab samplers retrieve sediment for analysis. Exciting camera work records lava bubbling up from beneath the seabed, scalding water gushing from undersea chimneys made of minerals, and glittering metal deposits on the seafloor, as well as an undreamed of wealth of marine creatures. On the deepest seabed new species are being discovered all the time.

Radar

Radar was invented simultaneously in Britain and Germany before World War II, when both countries were looking for ways of detecting enemy aircraft and ships before they could be seen. Radar bounces radio signals off a target. When the signals bounce back, they indicate the presence of obstructions such as rocks, even in dense fog. A radar screen aboard ship helps the navigator plot a safe course.

① ② ③ ④ ⑤

Seafloor samples

A water sampler is lowered to the seabed. Its bottles are operated at precise intervals as the device is lowered, giving a picture of a "slice" of the sea. This allows scientists to record the temperature and salinity of seawater, and to find out more about how currents work. Samples of sediment are taken from the seabed by dredging or vacuuming devices. Sediments are analyzed for their mineral content. One day it may be possible to mine valuable metals from the seabed.

Underwater exploration

Today's explorers probe into the ocean in pressurized suits like the Jim Suit (6), and submersibles such as Trieste (4), Sea-Link (1), Tech Diver (7), and Bathysphere (2). They take pictures with a deep-sea camera (3) and collect samples for analysis with a water sampler (5). A diver in an individual Jim Suit can descend 2,000 feet (610 m). The Bathysphere can dive to 3,034 feet (925 m), the Sea-Link to 3,280 feet (1,000 m), and the Trieste to the deepest place on Earth, 35,830 feet (10,920 m).

Navigation satellites

Navigation satellites are invaluable in helping ships keep exactly on course. The 24 satellites of the Global Positioning System (GPS) orbit at an altitude of 6,800 miles (11,000 km) above the Earth. The satellites constantly transmit the exact time along with information about their orbits. The GPS receiver onboard ship detects signals coming from at least three of the satellites, which arrive at slightly different times. From those times, a microchip inside the GPS receiver works out the ship's exact position.

Diver at work

A marine archaeologist explores a wreck. Diving is a dangerous business. Underwater, the pressure on the body increases, because of the weight of water above it. Air is supplied under the same pressure, so that the diver can breathe. At this pressure, nitrogen in the air supply also passes into the diver's bloodstream. If the diver surfaces too quickly, the sudden release of pressure causes bubbles of nitrogen to form in the blood and tissues. This painful condition, called decompression sickness, or the bends, can be fatal.

ARCTIC OCEAN

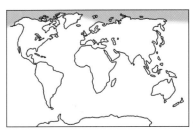

The North Pole is the most northerly point on Earth. The Arctic Circle is an imaginary line drawn around the pole at 66 degrees 30 minutes' north latitude. The Arctic Ocean lies inside the circle. The world's smallest ocean, it is frozen most of the year. When the ice begins to break up in spring it forms huge ice fields called floes. Part of the ocean never melts, but is locked in a vast icecap around the North Pole.

Newly broken off from the icecap, icebergs head for the Atlantic, on the Labrador Current. They are not always white—Arctic icebergs can be greenish blue or almost black, depending on the soil and debris that is frozen into them. Around the edge of the icecap is pack ice—it breaks and melts in summer, then as temperatures plummet again in the winter, it freezes and is packed together into amazing shapes by the movement of waves and tides. About half the pack ice in the Arctic Ocean melts and freezes each year.

To the North Pole

Explorers trying to reach the North Pole faced icebergs weighing up to 1.5 million tons, and the danger of superstructure icing —when a ship is encrusted in ice, it is likely to capsize. In 1875, Sir Allen Young's ship *Pandora* was thwarted by the ice. Commander Robert Peary of the U.S. Navy eventually became the first explorer to trek across the ice to the North Pole in 1909.

Arctic peoples

A good mode of travel in the long Arctic winter is the snowmobile, a small motorized vehicle on skis. The peoples of the Arctic include the Inuits (Eskimos) of Greenland, North America, and northeast Asia, the Aleuts of Alaska, the Yakuts and Chukchee of Russia, and the Sami (Lapps) of Scandinavia. Many lead a traditional way of life, hunting fish, seals, and whales, or herding reindeer. Others work in scientific research stations or in the oil industry. Large deposits of oil have been discovered offshore. Artificial islands have been built for rigs to stand on and the oil is removed by pipeline.

Midnight Sun

In midsummer, the Arctic day lasts for 24 hours, and the land within the Arctic Circle is known as the Land of the Midnight Sun. The ice sheet shrinks. On land, snow melts to reveal the tundra, a land of scrubby plants that burst into bloom over the short summer months. After barely 50 days, winter creeps back again. The ice sheet spreads and in the freezing winds, temperatures can drop to -58°F (-50°C). The Arctic midwinter is dark around the clock, with the Sun staying below the horizon.

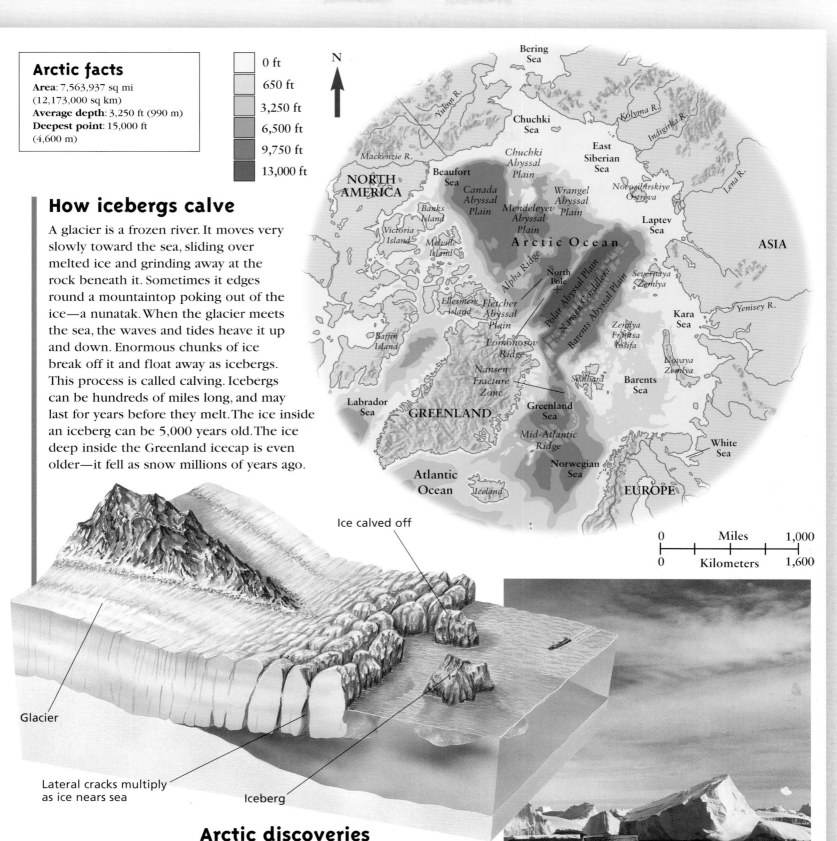

Arctic facts
Area: 7,563,937 sq mi
(12,173,000 sq km)
Average depth: 3,250 ft (990 m)
Deepest point: 15,000 ft
(4,600 m)

0 ft
650 ft
3,250 ft
6,500 ft
9,750 ft
13,000 ft

N

Bering
Sea

Yukon R.

Chuchki
Sea

Kolyma R.

Indigirka R.

Chuchki
Abyssal
Plain

East
Siberian
Sea

Mackenzie R.

Lena R.

Beaufort
Sea

**NORTH
AMERICA**

Canada
Abyssal
Plain

Wrangel
Abyssal
Plain

*Novosibirskiye
Ostrova*

Banks
Island

Mendeleyev
Abyssal
Plain

Laptev
Sea

ASIA

Victoria
Island

A r c t i c   O c e a n

Melville
Island

Alpha Ridge

North
Pole

Polar Abyssal Plain

Severnaya
Zemlya

Ellesmere
Island

Fletcher
Abyssal
Plain

Nansen Cordillera

Barents Abyssal Plain

Kara
Sea

Yenisey R.

Baffin
Island

Lomonosov
Ridge

Zemlya
Frantsa
Iosifa

Nansen
Fracture
Zone

Svalbard

Novaya
Zemlya

Labrador
Sea

Greenland
Sea

Barents
Sea

GREENLAND

Mid-Atlantic
Ridge

White
Sea

Norwegian
Sea

**Atlantic
Ocean**

Iceland

EUROPE

How icebergs calve

A glacier is a frozen river. It moves very
slowly toward the sea, sliding over
melted ice and grinding away at the
rock beneath it. Sometimes it edges
round a mountaintop poking out of the
ice—a nunatak. When the glacier meets
the sea, the waves and tides heave it up
and down. Enormous chunks of ice
break off it and float away as icebergs.
This process is called calving. Icebergs
can be hundreds of miles long, and may
last for years before they melt. The ice
inside an iceberg can be 5,000 years old. The ice
deep inside the Greenland icecap is even
older—it fell as snow millions of years ago.

Ice calved off

0	Miles	1,000
0	Kilometers	1,600

Glacier

Lateral cracks multiply
as ice nears sea

Iceberg

Arctic discoveries

Explorers reached the North Pole over the ice
in 1909, but in 1958, the U.S. nuclear submarine
Nautilus became the first ship to reach the
North Pole. It traveled right under the icecap,
finally proving that there is no Arctic continent.
Exploration of the Arctic's four
ocean basins continues
today. As Russian,
American, and Canadian
ships cross the ocean, they
are accompanied by
icebreakers, which double
as research vessels
studying weather and the
movements of the ice.

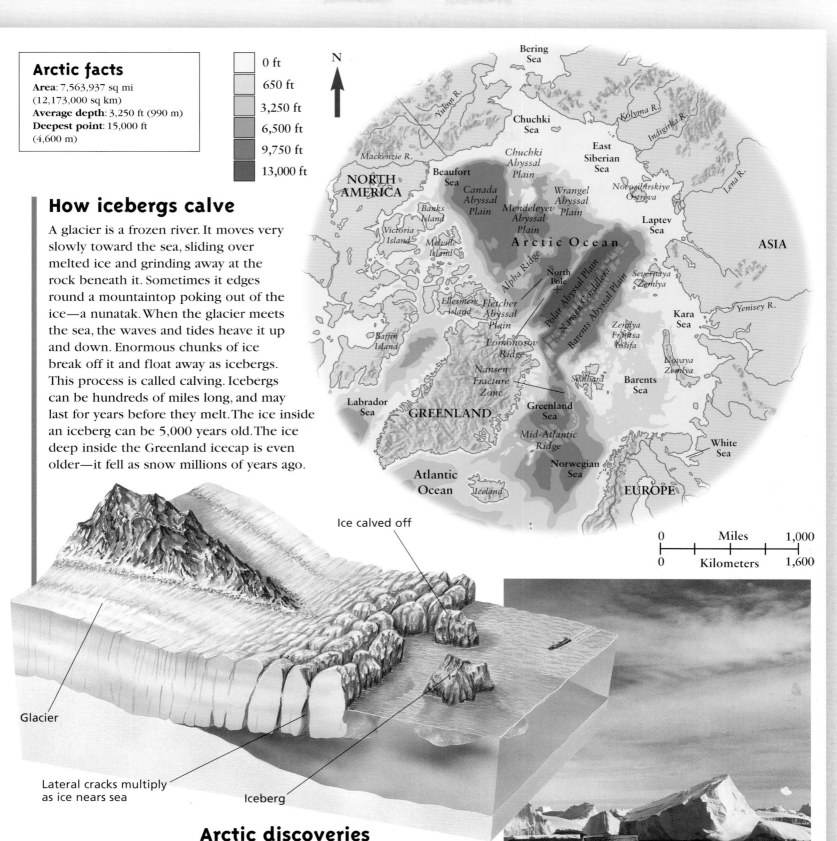

35

ANTARCTIC OCEAN

The Atlantic, Indian, and Pacific oceans meet south of latitude 55 degrees to form the Antarctic Ocean. The world's fourth-largest ocean surrounds the ice-bound continent of Antarctica at the South Pole.

In winter, more than half of the ocean freezes over, and towering icebergs and treacherous storms threaten shipping in bitter winds. The lowest temperature in the world has been recorded here: –128.6°F (–89.2°C), yet fossils of trees, dinosaurs and mammals found here prove that Antarctica was once an ice-free continent.

Research stations in the Antarctic monitor the ozone hole in Earth's upper atmosphere, which has been caused by chemicals such as chlorofluorocarbons (CFCs) in refrigerators and aerosols. The hole lets in dangerously strong ultraviolet rays from the Sun. Almost three-quarters of the world's fresh water is locked up in Antarctic ice. If it were to melt, the continent of Antarctica, released from under its weight, would rise by 650-1,000 feet (200-300 m). The world's sea level would rise by 200 feet (60 m), causing flooding around the globe and submerging many major cities. A rise in temperature could also threaten the growth of plankton and kelp, with disastrous effects for the food chain.

Antarctic wildlife

In winter, Emperor penguins breed on the ice. The female lays a single egg and the male incubates it between his feet. When it hatches, the parents take turns caring for the chick and hunting for fish. The cold Antarctic waters teem with life. An upwelling of nutrients around the coast feeds phytoplankton, which in turn feed shrimplike krill. Swarms of krill turn coastal waters red during the day and glowing blue at night. Phytoplankton form the base of the ocean's food chain.

Scientific research

The only way to get supplies to scientists working at research stations in Antarctica is to fly them there, but for several months each year winds are so strong and temperatures so low that not even a helicopter can land. Deposits of oil, metals, and coal have been discovered offshore, but none has been exploited. Instead, this frozen wilderness has been dedicated to scientific research—42 nations around the world have signed a treaty to protect it.

Frozen wilderness

The Antarctic is even colder and icier than the Arctic. Much of the land is pushed below sea level by the massive weight of the ice, which is 15,750 feet (4,800 m) thick at its deepest point. The icecap spreads across the ocean, shrinking in summer and expanding in winter, when the sea is choked with icebergs calving from (breaking off) its edge. The currents of the Antarctic are driven by freezing winds, called the roaring forties, the furious fifties, and the shrieking sixties, after the latitudes in which they blow. The aurora australis—southern lights—flashes in the sky as magnetic forces pull particles from the Sun to stream into Earth's atmosphere.

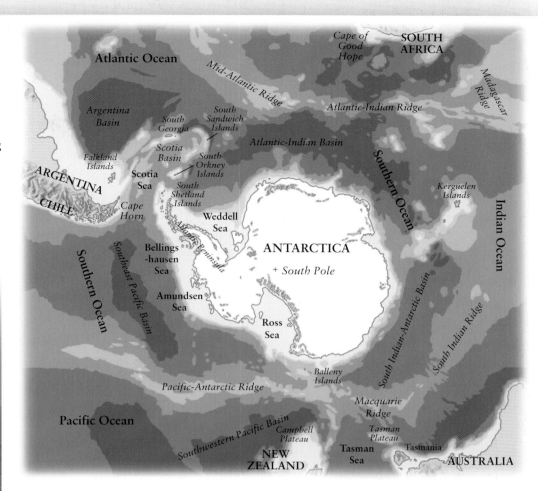

0 ft	
3,250 ft	
6,500 ft	
9,750 ft	
13,000 ft	
16,250 ft	

Miles 0 — 1,000
Kilometers 0 — 1,600

Antarctic facts

Area: 13,500,000 sq mi
(35,000,000 sq km)
Sea ice: 8,100,000 sq mi
(21,000,000 sq km) freeze in winter
Permanently frozen :
1,540,000 sq mi
(4,000,000 sq km)

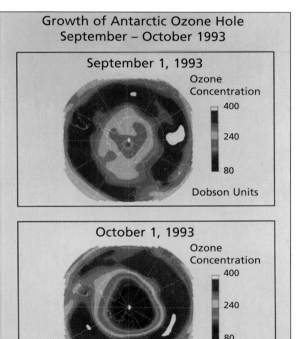

Growth of Antarctic Ozone Hole September – October 1993

September 1, 1993

Ozone Concentration
400
240
80
Dobson Units

October 1, 1993

Ozone Concentration
400
240
80
Dobson Units

The ozone hole

A hole as big as a continent has formed in the upper atmosphere over Antarctica and is continuing to grow. It is the result of damage by chemicals to the ozone layer, the thin layer of the gas ozone (O_3) that shields life on Earth from the Sun's harmful ultraviolet rays. These false-color satellite images show a dramatic decrease in ozone concentration over one month, between September and October 1993.

ATLANTIC OCEAN

The Atlantic Ocean began to form 150 million years ago when movements of the Earth's crust separated the Americas from Europe and Africa. The Atlantic is the world's second largest ocean, covering about one fifth of the Earth's surface.

Its arms form the Caribbean, North, Baltic, and Mediterranean Seas. The coasts of the Americas in the west and Europe and Africa in the east drop underwater to gently sloping continental shelves, then the ocean floor dives to deep basins and trenches. Running down the middle in an S-shape across the equator is the Mid-Atlantic Ridge, one of the great cracks in the Earth's crust. The two plates at either side of it are being pushed apart, and the ocean is growing by about 1 $^3/4$ inches (4 cm) a year. Molten rock from deep under the Earth oozes up through this crack and cools, building ridges of seabed mountains. Where they rise above the surface, they form volcanic islands such as the Azores. Powerful ocean currents in the Atlantic are caused by the mixing of cold water from the polar seas with warm waters from the tropics. The Benguela and Malvinas Currents flow from the Antarctic, the Labrador and East Greenland Currents from the Arctic. Warm waters are carried from the tropics by the Gulf Stream, the Brazil Current, and the North Atlantic Drift.

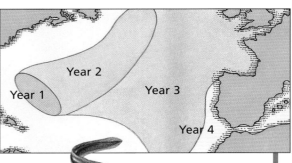

Year 1
Year 2
Year 3
Year 4

Green turtle

Green turtles live off the coast of Brazil, but spend much of their lives on the move. They swim through the South Atlantic waters to lay their eggs on Ascension Island. When the young turtles have hatched out, the families swim back again, making a journey of 1,750 miles (2,800 km). Turtles have streamlined bodies and flipper-shaped front legs. They use their back feet as rudders for steering, and come to the surface to breathe.

Sargasso Sea

The Sargasso Sea is a vast area of calm water in the north central Atlantic where ocean currents carry warm water down to great depths. Eels migrate here from America and Europe to breed on the seabed and die. Their eggs hatch into larvae, which live and feed among the Sargassum weed that drifts near the surface. As the larvae grow into elvers (young eels), they catch the Gulf Stream and drift northward. Four years after hatching they reach the same American and European streams that their parents left.

The Gulf Stream

This computer-enhanced satellite image shows (in red) the Gulf Stream, a warm ocean current that begins in the western Caribbean Sea and sweeps round the coast of Florida. From there it travels up the eastern seaboard of the U.S. and spreads across the Atlantic, washing the coasts of Britain. Thanks to its warming influence on the climate, tropical plants can survive in gardens in southwest England, which are on the same latitude as that where the *Titanic* was sunk by an iceberg. If global warming melts ice caps and increases rainfall, the added fresh water could disrupt the Gulf Stream, leaving southwest England to be gripped by long Siberian winters.

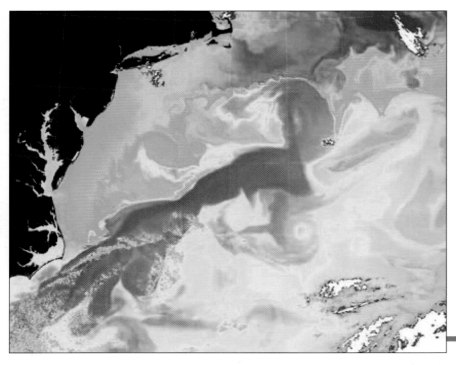

Mangrove swamps

The estuaries and coasts of West Africa are fringed with mangrove trees. These unusual trees are able to survive in seawater because their succulent leaves excrete excess salt. The mangrove's remarkable roots arch from the trunk of the tree and spread out to colonize the mud in which the trees thrive. The intricate root network encourages and traps silt, forming a swamp that slowly moves the land further into the sea. The roots provide shelter for many kinds of wildlife, including fish that can hop across dry land called mudskippers, and crocodiles. In some regions, mangroves are cleared to make way for fish farms. Coastal erosion and loss of wildlife is the result.

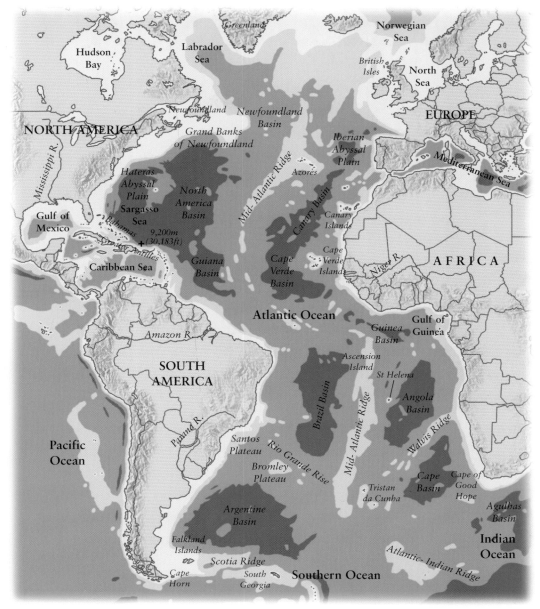

An island is born

Some Atlantic islands, like the British Isles, have broken away from a continent. But many of the islands in the Atlantic are volcanoes, formed when molten rock bubbled out of the crack in Earth's crust that is called the Mid-Atlantic Ridge.

The island of Surtsey (right) is a volcano that rose from the sea close to Iceland in 1965. Great clouds of steam and gas billowed into the sky as the island rose in a drama of ice and fire, only to disappear again the following year. The illustration below shows how a volcanic island is formed.

0 ft	
3,250 ft	
9,750 ft	
16,250 ft	

N

	Miles	
0		2,000
0	Kilometers	3,200

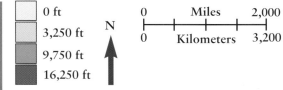

Atlantic facts

Area: 31,450,000 sq mi
(81,500,000 sq km)
Average depth: 11,800 ft (3,600 m)
Deepest point: 28,200 ft (8,600 m)
in Puerto Rico Trench

PEOPLE & HISTORY

ATLANTIC OCEAN

The Vikings crossed the Atlantic well ahead of Christopher Columbus, the famous Italian navigator who sailed to the Caribbean in 1492. He was searching for a trade route to the East Indies, but landed instead in the Americas. During the next centuries, huge waves of conquerors and immigrants sailed across the Atlantic to settle in the New World. They fought with the native inhabitants to take their land, and wiped out many more by spreading European diseases.

Life at sea was hard. Many perished in shipwrecks or at the hands of pirates. Countless captives died crammed in slave ships. Sailors survived on boiled turtle or dry biscuits full of maggots—in desperation they even ate leather. To cross the Atlantic westward they caught the trade winds; the westerlies (blowing from the west) carried them back east. But lying on the equator is a band of mirror-flat water called the doldrums—here a ship could drift for weeks without a breath of wind.

Today the Atlantic's northern shores are studded with great cities and huge ports such as New York in the U.S., and Liverpool and Lisbon in Europe. Its fishing villages, set in rugged scenery, earn new income from tourists. The southern hemisphere has fewer great cities. Here many coastal people lead a traditional way of life, fishing for their food. Many mid-Atlantic islands serve as stop-off points and ports.

The Spanish Main

The Spanish Main meant the mainland of America, which had been conquered by Spain. It was a great lure for pirates, who ambushed ships that were bound for Europe laden with gold and jewels. Mary Read and Anne Bonny disguised themselves as men to become pirates in the 1700s. Bonny fell in love with Read, thinking she was a man. Then both revealed their secrets and they became great friends. When their ship was captured, the women escaped the death penalty for piracy because they were both pregnant.

Viking longboat

The Vikings were brilliant ship-builders and navigators. They set sail from their homes in Norway, Sweden, and Denmark from the 900s A.D. and by 1000 A.D. had sailed from Greenland to Newfoundland. Their vessels were wooden longboats, ships with one square sail and several pairs of oars for rowing when there was no wind. These fast-moving craft were used for raiding trips—many Viking leaders grew wealthy by plundering villages along the coasts and rivers of Europe.

Slave ship

The slave trade began in the 1400s when Europeans sailed to Africa to buy captured men, women, and children, and shipped them across the Atlantic to work in European colonies. Slaves were chained on the boat and kept in terrible conditions. Between 1701 and 1810, more than a million Africans died of suffocation, starvation or disease during the voyage, which could last up to ten weeks. The trade in humans lasted until the early years of the 1800s.

The unsinkable sinks

The hull of the *Titanic* had watertight compartments designed to make her unsinkable. But on her maiden voyage in 1912, the ship was sunk by a huge iceberg off Newfoundland, with the loss of 1,513 lives. The wreck was finally located in 1985 by a team using remote-controlled video cameras. Today Ice Patrol aircraft warn of icebergs, but they are still a hazard to shipping.

Exploring the depths

Jacques Cousteau (1910-1997), below, and his colleague Emile Gagnan opened up the modern era of underwater exploration in 1942 when they invented the aqualung or SCUBA—the self-contained underwater breathing apparatus. The aqualung liberated divers from heavy helmets, weighted boots and hoses that fed air from above. Cousteau, from France, was one of the greatest marine explorers of all time. During his long career he wrote books and made many films and T.V. programs about the deep.

Sea defenses

Erosion—wearing away by waves and wind—threatens coastlines and settlements on both sides of the North Atlantic. Here, a mechanical digger begins to build a sea wall at Weymouth, Dorset, on the south coast of England. In the U.S., many millions of dollars have been spent in rebuilding Miami's beaches with imported sand to preserve luxury holiday resorts and homes. The erection of fences that keep beaches stable and other sea defenses, may be temporarily effective, but often causes worse problems of erosion elsewhere along the coast.

Heroine of the seas

In a daunting trial of endurance, courage, and skill, British sailor Ellen MacArthur, 24, thrilled the world by finishing second in the Vendée Globe race 2000-1, sailing single-handedly around the world in less than 95 days. On the voyage she ate freeze-dried food, watched albatrosses, read *Harry Potter*, and missed her dog. Her most dangerous moment came when she was almost sunk by an iceberg. But the worst thing that happened, she said, was getting off the boat at the end. Ellen bought her first boat when she was 13, saving up for it with her school lunch money.

ECONOMY

ATLANTIC OCEAN

Trade across the Atlantic began in the 1600s, when Europeans shipped supplies to the new colonies, bringing back furs and tobacco. They also sold slaves to American plantation owners in exchange for cotton and sugar. In the 1800s, thousands of people immigrated to North America by sea, which opened a trade route. Today, ships carry huge loads of coal, iron ore, timber, wheat, and oil across the Atlantic.

Atlantic waters are among the richest fishing grounds in the world. But today, because of overfishing, cod and hake, which once teemed around fishing boats off Labrador, are now a threatened species. Off Canada, Scotland and Norway, salmon are raised in cages in the sea. The fish are protected and fed. In shallow waters off France and Spain, mussels are farmed in beds that fill with seawater. Meanwhile, in the South Atlantic, many people still use traditional methods of netting just enough fish to feed their families. One quarter of the ocean's catch still goes into animal feeds or fertilizers.

Salt mine

This salt mine is on a South Atlantic beach in Namibia, southern Africa. Here seawater is fed into shallow pools. When the water evaporates in the Sun, the salt that is left behind is scraped into a gigantic heap, from which it can be loaded onto trucks and carted off for sale and export. Some minerals are actually mined under the sea. Close to the Namibian shore, diamonds are sifted from sand dredged from the seabed.

Winter sun

The Canary Islands belong to Spain but lie in the Atlantic off the coast of West Africa. The islands' beaches are black volcanic rock—to make them more appealing to tourists, thousands of tons of white sand have been imported from the Sahara. Tourism is the islands' most important business.

New York

Henry Hudson discovered a magnificent natural harbor in 1609 at the mouth of the river named in his honor (see satellite picture above). The city of New York sprang up there, and today it is the Atlantic's largest and busiest port. Many miles of docks along the shore have deep-water channels that can accept giant supertankers and container ships.

North Atlantic fishing

Because fish stocks are running low, rules limit the size of a boat's catch and the number of days it can go to sea, but they are difficult to enforce. The holes in fishing nets must be big enough to allow younger fish to swim through—but many are still caught and killed. Long drift nets break free and go on "ghost fishing"—killing fish, dolphins, and seals. Poorer nations sell fishing rights to richer ones, so there is not enough left to feed the locals. Yet scientists believe with better management, the fishing industry could easily provide enough food for all.

The polluted sea

The *Torrey Canyon* ran aground off southwest England in 1967, spilling oil that coated beaches and killed wildlife. A major pollution incident such as this causes outrage, but few realize that each year we pour billions of tons of toxic waste into the Atlantic in the form of industrial and agricultural chemicals, garbage, and sewage. Coastal areas are heavily polluted and poisons entering the bodies of fish and shellfish work their way up the food chain to humans.

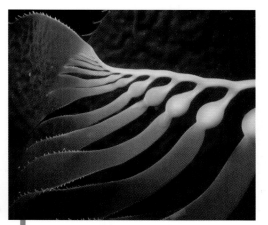

Whaling

There were once whaling stations on the North Atlantic coast of the U.S. Vast numbers of whales were killed and taken there to be processed, and many species were brought close to extinction. The humpback, the bowhead, and the northern right whale are still in danger. Despite an international ban in the 1980s, Norway and Japan continue whaling. Here activists from Greenpeace stage a protest under the bows of a massive whaling vessel.

Giant kelp

Forests of giant kelp grow in coastal South Atlantic waters. Apart from providing food and shelter for sea creatures, kelp has long been useful to humans. Dried and reduced to ashes, this seaweed was once used in glass-making and the manufacture of soap. Today kelp is farmed for use as a dietary supplement and is also a valuable fertilizer.

NORTH ATLANTIC SHORES

ATLANTIC OCEAN

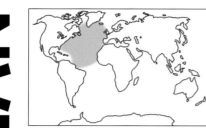

The icy Labrador Current sweeps down the Canadian coast from the Arctic and meets the warm Gulf Stream near Newfoundland. The difference in temperature causes heavy sea fogs. Mountainous icebergs drift south in the cold current, presenting additional hazards to shipping.

About 90 percent of the ocean's fish live in the shallow waters of the continental shelves that surround the land, feeding on the plankton that live there. The Labrador Sea used to seethe with cod, a fish that also eats crabs, lobsters, sea urchins, and squid, and can grow to 5 feet (1.5 m) long. Much of the catch was salted and dried in the traditional fashion, and cod was cheap. Today it has been fished so extensively that it is scarce and expensive. The two largest islands of the North Atlantic are Iceland and Greenland, the largest island in the world. Most of Greenland is covered in an ice sheet up to 2 miles (3 km) thick, and the country has no more inhabitants than a large town. In Iceland, hot springs of salty water offer the population cheap heating from a renewable source that does not pollute. Spring water is also used to heat greenhouses, so fresh vegetables can be grown all year.

Fishing rods, nets, and traps

There are many ways to catch a fish. From a beach, a rod and line (1) can be used, and with a small boat, a Rockwall trap can be used (2), a fence (3), or a beach seine (4). Lobsters are caught in lobster pots (5), dropped overboard and marked with a buoy. Fyke nets (6) are placed at the entrance to a current and larger boats use a cast net (7) or a gill net (8). Dredges (9) collect shellfish from the muddy seabed.

Trapping

The Hudson's Bay Company was founded in 1670 to trade in furs. Pelts from animals such as the polar bear and the Arctic fox were luxurious novelties in Europe, and were shipped back on the same boats that brought supplies, tools, and seeds to the European settlers in North America. Today the historic Hudson's Bay Company is still Canada's biggest fur company, though it also sells general goods through its department stores and owns interests in offshore oil and gas. Meanwhile, fur trading has been restricted under conservation measures. The trapping of Arctic animals is strictly limited to licensed Inuit hunters.

Rich feeding grounds

The cold seas around Baffin Island in the northwest Atlantic are an area of upwelling, with mineral-rich seawater rising from the ocean floor to supply nutrients for the whole food chain. Many seabirds migrate to these rich feeding grounds to breed, including the Arctic terns flocking in the background. They make the greatest migratory journey of all animals—flying from halfway round the globe in the Antarctic. The Atlantic puffin (inset) nests on the clifftops, but stays out at sea in the winter. Puffins fly strongly on fast-beating wings, and swim underwater to chase fish and eels, which they carry to their chicks in their beaks. The puffin makes its nest in a burrow lined with grass and feathers.

The hot springs of Iceland

Every year thousands of people visit Iceland's Blue Lagoon to swim in its warm waters and benefit from their famous healing powers. Hot springs bubble up, heated by magma deep under the Earth, to fill the lagoon with mineral-rich seawater. People can bathe here even when snow covers the surrounding hills. In the background, a power station pumps the nearly boiling spring water directly to people's homes. Hot water and heating is supplied this way to 85 percent of Icelanders.

Whale tooth

Sperm whales have teeth only in the lower jaw, and in the days before the international ban on whale hunting, these teeth were as prized as elephants' tusks. Whale ivories were kept as trophies by hunters and could fetch a good price on the market. Sailors spent long winter evenings scratching designs into the ivories with the point of a sharp knife—a form of art called scrimshaw. This 8-inch (20-cm)-long tooth has been engraved by the hunter, and shows his whaling ship and the sweetheart he left onshore.

Traditional hunting

Most Greenlanders are descended from native Inuits (Eskimos) and immigrant Danes. (Greenland belongs to Denmark.) Many of the inhabitants of this vast ice-bound isle lead a traditional way of life, hunting whales and narwhals. Seal-hunters take to the icy water in tiny kayaks, boats made of animal skin stretched over a wooden frame. International laws that ban commercial hunting of seals and whales do not apply to native peoples who need to hunt animals for their meat and skins.

45

SOUTH ATLANTIC SHORES

ATLANTIC OCEAN

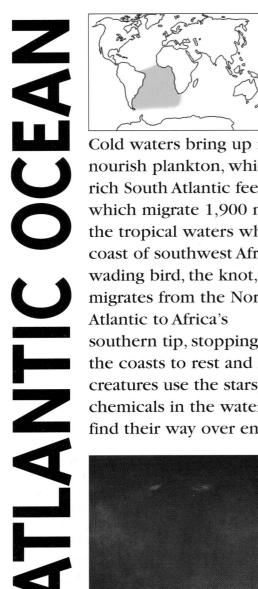

The ocean current that pushes northward around the coast of Africa is cold, which means that moisture does not rise from the sea and fall on the land as rain. The result is a band of sandy desert, the Namib, running the length of the southwest African coast.

Cold waters bring up minerals from the ocean depths to nourish plankton, which in turn provide food for fish. The rich South Atlantic feeding grounds attract baleen whales, which migrate 1,900 miles (3,000 km) in summer from the tropical waters where they breed. Seals come to the coast of southwest Africa to breed. The world's smallest wading bird, the knot, migrates from the North Atlantic to Africa's southern tip, stopping along the coasts to rest and feed. Sea creatures use the stars, the Sun, and chemicals in the water to help them find their way over enormous distances.

Blue whale

The largest animal that lives on Earth is the blue whale. It has an average length of 85 feet (26 m) and weighs around 110 tons. Whales can reach such a huge size because the water supports the weight of their bodies. If a whale is beached on land, the weight of its body crushes its internal organs and kills it. Whales breathe through a blowhole on top of their heads. When the whale surfaces, it blows out stale air as a spout of spray, breathes in quickly and dives again.

Shackleton and the *Endurance*

The Irish explorer Ernest Shackleton (1874-1922) made four courageous voyages to explore the South Atlantic and icy Antarctic Oceans. He was a member of Captain Scott's Antarctic expedition, he located the magnetic South Pole, and he climbed Mount Erebus, Antarctica's only mountain and an active volcano. In 1914, he commanded an expedition to cross the Antarctic, but his ship, the *Endurance*, was crushed by ice on the Weddell Sea. Heroically, Shackleton made an 800-mile (1,300-km) journey in an open boat to get help for his stranded crew. He died in the Antarctic on board the *Quest* in 1922.

Jangadas

The traditional Brazilian fishing boat is called a jangada. It is a raft made of logs lashed together with twine, and has a triangular sail. The craft is moved on rollers down the beach and into the sea. The fisherman straps himself to the deck to sleep as the jangada sails out by night up to 30 miles (50 km) off the coast. At dawn he makes his catch, then takes advantage of the onshore winds to sail back home.

The Falklands War

British Marines on HMS *Hermes* in the South Atlantic prepare to board a Sea King helicopter, which will take them to the Falkland Islands. The Falklands War began in 1981, when Argentina invaded the islands, a British colony off its shores. Argentina claimed ownership of the islands, which it calls Las Malvinas. In the ensuing conflict over 1,000 British and Argentine soldiers lost their lives. Argentina surrendered in 1982 and the islands were returned to British rule.

Flamingos

Huge flocks of flamingos feed in the muddy bays along the shoreline of West Africa. Holding the tips of their beaks upside-down, they wade through the shallows on their long pink legs, pumping the water with their tongues and filtering out tiny crustaceans with comblike devices in their beaks, called lamellae.

Fur seal

Fur seals live in the cold Atlantic waters off the Falkland Islands, feeding on fish and squid, and coming ashore to rest and breed at traditional sites called rookeries. Eared seals such as the fur seal have torpedo-shaped bodies like true seals, but their flippers are bigger and more powerful. They swim by rowing with their front flippers and pushing with their rear flippers, like a fish uses its tail. On land they shuffle along, tucking their rear flippers under their body and propping themselves up on their front pair. On land they are clumsy movers, but in water they are fast and very graceful swimmers.

Rough seas at Cape Horn

Swirling currents, gale-force westerly winds, and icebergs make for treacherous seas around Cape Horn, at the southernmost tip of South America. The Dutch navigator Willem Schouten was the first to sail round the Cape in 1616, and named it for his birthplace, Hoorn in The Netherlands. During the time of sailing ships, hundreds of vessels were wrecked while "rounding the Horn," and countless sailors lost their lives in the tumultuous seas. Today, ships can use the Panama Canal to avoid the Horn.

47

NORTH SEA & BALTIC

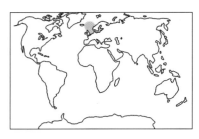

The North Sea lies between the British Isles and Scandinavia and is linked to the Baltic by a passage called the Skagerrak between Norway and Denmark. These seas were once land, but when the last ice age ended 10,000 years ago, meltwater cut Britain off from Europe.

The North Sea is kept above freezing by the warm Gulf Stream current, but the Baltic freezes over in winter. Its waters are brackish (less salty). Fresh water flows into it from rivers, and not much oxygen-rich salt water enters through the Skaggerak. The Baltic has hardly any tides, and its water is replaced only once every 50 years. Some areas of the sea support little life.

On the bed of the North Sea, mud, sand, and gravel left behind by glaciers have been shaped into banks and trenches by strong currents. It is one of the busiest waterways in the world, with a complicated network of shipping lanes routed around oil and gas fields, fishing grounds, sand and gravel mines, and military exercise zones. The North Sea's vigorous tides and currents ensure that its nutrient-rich waters are well-mixed, making it a good feeding ground for fish. But overfishing and pollution are threatening fish stocks. Ships in the North Sea release over 88,000 tons of oil every year when cleaning out their tanks—the equivalent of a major oil spill. Industry discharges thousands of tons of heavy metals such as mercury, cadmium, and lead into the sea through smokestacks or by pumping effluent into rivers.

The Thames Barrier

Britain's capital, London, is at risk of flooding from freak surge tides—low pressure over the North Sea causes a rise in sea levels. Combined with a northerly wind and heavy rain, a hump of water is forced through the English channel and up the Thames estuary. Over 200 people drowned in the city during the last great flood of 1953. The Thames Barrier is designed to protect the city from floods. It has four gates that rest on the riverbed when not in service. When raised, they are the height of a five-story building.

North Sea riches

Deep below the surface, trapped between layers of rock, lie pools of oil and pockets of gas. These are fossil fuels that formed millions of years ago from the decayed bodies of sea animals and plants. The discovery of oil and gas under the North Sea in the 1960s made Norway and Britain much richer. Thousands of people work in the oil industry, building rigs and pipelines, and refining the crude oil to make gasoline. A steel framework supports this rig beneath the sea, and the oil is brought to land by pipeline. Workers reach the rig by helicopter, landing on its helideck. North Sea gas and oil supply 30 percent of Europe's energy needs.

North Sea and Baltic facts

Area: North Sea 220,000 sq mi (570,000 sq km)
                 Baltic 162,000 sq mi (420,000 sq km)

Average depth: North Sea 308 ft (94 m)
                 Baltic 217 ft (66 m)

Maximum depth: North Sea 2,395 ft (730 m)
                 Baltic 1,506 ft (459 m)

Miles	
0	500
0	800
Kilometers	

N

0 ft
165 ft
325 ft
650 ft
975 ft
Over 1,650 ft

Coasts at risk

Strong tides and storm winds lash at the east coast of Britain, eroding the cliffs and causing dramatic landfalls. Here, waves have toppled a chalet in Norfolk from its perch and sent it crashing on to the beach. On the other side of the North Sea, The Netherlands are sinking. The Dutch have battled against the danger of flooding for centuries. They have built dikes and huge barrier dams to hold back the sea, and have pumped water off large areas of land to claim them. About a third of The Netherlands lies below sea level and has been reclaimed. The drained land, called polder, is very fertile and is used mainly for agriculture, including the famous bulb fields.

Baltic treasure

Amber is solidified tree resin. It is prized in jewelry and has been a source of wealth around the Baltic for 4,000 years. Translucent nuggets of this precious substance may be yellow or deep orange-gold, and occasionally have an insect trapped inside. Amber is mined from the greenish sand on Baltic shores, and also collected in nets in the surf. The Baltic also has important herring fisheries, but they are badly affected by pollution. Sewage and wash-off from farm chemicals cause eutrophication—a bloom of algae on top of the water. When the algae die, they sink and decompose. Then oxygen levels near the seabed fall sharply, and fish suffocate. In the Baltic, where water mixes slowly, this is a serious problem.

Shipping

Rotterdam, in The Netherlands, (below) is the world's largest port, handling 316 million tons of cargo a year. It is also Europe's leading container terminal. Built on the mouths of the Waal and Lek rivers (see satellite photo), it has grown into a world-class center for oil refining, manufacturing, and shipbuilding. Hamburg is another major North Sea port, while the Baltic has Helsinki, Stockholm, and Copenhagen. In winter, icebreakers free up frozen Baltic ports to allow ships to enter. The Nord-Ostsee Canal, across northern Germany, opened in 1895, spares ships the dangerous passage through the Skagerrak and a journey of 350 miles (560 km).

Rotterdam

MEDITERRANEAN SEA

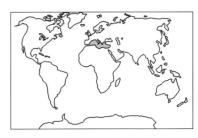

The Mediterranean Sea divides Europe from Africa, and is connected with the Atlantic Ocean at the narrow Strait of Gibraltar in the west. The Black Sea feeds into it through the Bosporus in the northeast, and in the southeast the Suez Canal leads to the Red Sea.

The Mediterranean's tides are gentle, but its currents are complex. Water evaporates in the hot summer sun, making the Mediterranean saltier. As the water cools in winter, it becomes denser and sinks, flowing out through the Strait of Gibraltar into the deeper Atlantic. A less salty stream of water is drawn above it into the Mediterranean. Mediterranean winds include the wintry mistral, which blows down the Rhone valley to Marseille, and the sirocco, which rises off the Sahara and blows north to scorch Italy.

The large islands of the Mediterranean depend on fishing, farming, and tourism. They include Sicily and Sardinia, Crete, Corsica, Cyprus, and Malta. Hundreds of small islands are scattered in the deep blue seas around Greece.

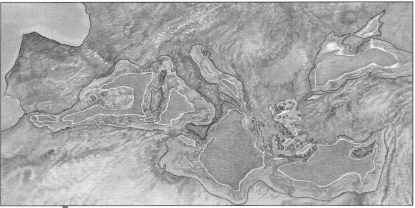

When the sea was a desert

Earth scientists believe that the Mediterranean dried up and refilled about a dozen times as the European and African continents joined and then parted at the Strait of Gibraltar around seven million years ago. A layer of salts more than 1.2 miles (2 km) thick on the seabed indicates that six million years ago, the Mediterranean was a desert dotted with salty ponds. Then five million years ago, continental drift caused the Strait to reopen, creating a massive waterfall from the Atlantic. It refilled the Mediterranean in 100 years.

Ashqelon, city of the sea

Just west of modern Ashqelon on Israel's coast are the ruins of the ancient city of Ashqelon. For 5,000 years it was one of the great Mediterranean seaports—today much of the site has been claimed by the rising sea. Archaeologists have excavated many treasures here, including a graveyard with the skeletons of over 1,000 dogs.

The Suez Canal

Opened in 1869, the Suez Canal joins the Mediterranean Sea to the Gulf of Suez. It allows ships to pass directly into the Red Sea, and from there to the Indian Ocean, saving a journey around Africa. This important waterway has been the focus of conflict in the Middle East. Egypt claimed ownership of the canal in 1956, and as a result was attacked by Israel, Britain, and France. Further wars with Israel closed the canal from 1967 to 1975. Egypt has recently enlarged the canal to allow passage to huge supertankers carrying oil from the Gulf.

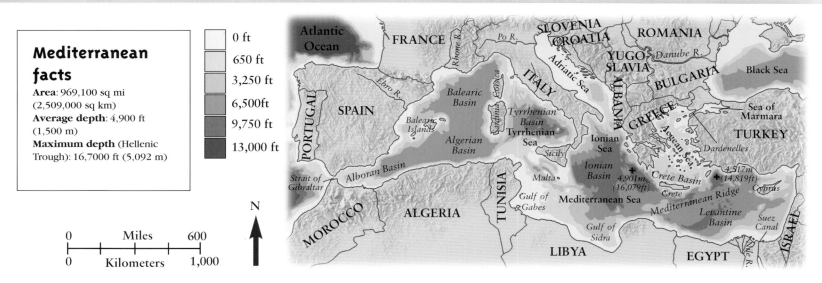

0 ft
650 ft
3,250 ft
6,500ft
9,750 ft
13,000 ft

N

Miles 600
Kilometers 1,000

Mediterranean volcanoes

The two plates that carry the European and African continents are drifting slowly towards each other. They squeeze and stretch the Earth's crust, triggering earthquakes and volcanoes across the Mediterranean. In 1470 B.C., a massive volcanic explosion on the Greek island of Thira ripped out the island's heart (see photo). Tsunami set off by the eruption may have wiped out the Minoan civilization on Crete. Italy's Mount Vesuvius had a famous eruption in 79 A.D., burying the town of Pompeii. Today on Sicily, Mount Etna rumbles. On the Lipari Islands, Mount Stromboli, affectionately called the "Lighthouse of the Mediterranean," hurls out fiery balls of magma almost continuously. Mount Lipari has not erupted since 525 A.D., but is not extinct, and could erupt again at any time.

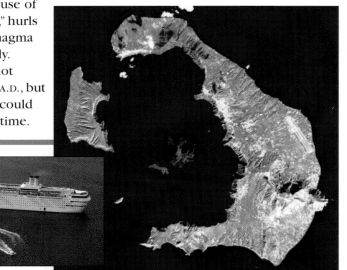

Europe's first empire

The Minoans were skilled architects and artists producing fabulous buildings and frescoes (wall paintings). The Minoan civilisation was named after Minos, the legendary king of the island. This civilisation flourished from 2500 B.C. till about 1500 B.C. when it was either destroyed by a tsunami, caused by the eruption of Thira, or by the Mycenaeans, invaders from the Greek mainland. The Minoans were great seatraders who set up sea ports as bases throughout the Aegean, from Palestine to Greece and from Cyprus to Egypt.

Vacation playground

The warm climate, natural beauty, historic sights, and delicious food of the countries surrounding the Mediterranean draw a staggering number of the world's tourists each year. This puts added strain on the area's already overstretched sewage treatment systems and much of the sewage is pumped untreated into the sea. In some regions, the spread of hotels threatens the habitats of creatures such as turtles, which come ashore to lay their eggs on the beach. The Mediterranean is also a busy shipping route, which causes extra pollution to the area. Since the 1970s, Mediterranean countries have been making an effort to reduce pollution, but the development of better systems has been slow, and there is still a long way to go.

INLAND SEAS

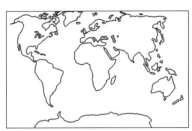

The three seas of Central Europe and Asia—the Black Sea, the Caspian Sea, and the Aral Sea—were once part of the same large body of water. Then sea levels fell and they became separate. Around 8,000 years ago, the waters of the Mediterranean rose and created a link to the Black Sea at the Bosporus.

Today these seas have a sorry tale to tell. During the 20th century when the countries to the north were part of the Soviet Union, large-scale industrialization polluted their waters. The fisheries in the Black Sea have collapsed, and there is little life there apart from massive blooms of jellyfish. The countries around the sea have been forced to adopt a conservation program. The Aral Sea is dying and choked with salt. The Caspian Sea, which began the century producing half the world's oil, suffered badly when the Soviet Union broke apart. Its filthy waters are now littered with rusting oil wells and the hulks of abandoned Soviet warships. Once salt was harvested from the sea, but even that is now contaminated by wastes from drilling and is no longer fit for human consumption.

The Danube delta

The second longest river in Europe, the Danube, rises in Germany's Black Forest and flows 1,770 miles (2,860 km) to enter the Black Sea in Romania in a swampy delta. The silt deposited by the river makes the surrounding plains fertile, and farmers grow corn, wheat, and grapes. The delta is a rich habitat for wildlife. Rare Dalmatian pelicans breed here, diving into the water to catch fish, but their numbers are threatened by hunting. Their territory is also being depleted as more land is drained for agriculture.

Istanbul

Istanbul was founded as Byzantium around 2,500 years ago, then renamed Constantinople. The great port of Istanbul and the Harbor of the Golden Horn stand on the Bosporus. This narrow waterway carries ships between the Black Sea and the Sea of Marmara, which leads into the Mediterranean Sea. The neck of water that joins the Sea of Marmara and the Mediterannean is called The Dardanelles. This was the site of the disastrous Gallipoli campaign of 1915 where over 10,000 ANZACS (Australia and New Zealand Army Corps) lost their lives.

Inland seas facts

Caspian Sea: 144,000 sq mi
(373,000 sq km)
Black Sea: 159,600 sq mi (413,360 sq km)
Aral Sea: 12,000 sq mi (31,080 sq km)

Sturgeon fishing

A fisherman on the Caspian Sea
(below) lands a sturgeon (below
right). The common sturgeon found
in the Mediterranean and the Atlantic
is not as highly prized as the beluga
sturgeon of the Caspian Sea. The
beluga can reach a length of 26 feet
(8 m) and weigh 3,300 pounds (1,500
kg). It is valued for its gleaming black
roe (eggs), which are salted to
preserve them, then sold as caviar,
one of the world's greatest and
most expensive delicacies.
Stocks of sturgeon in
the Caspian Sea have
plummeted due to pollution
and illegal poaching. A total ban on fishing—
as well as conservation measures to clean up
the sea—may be necessary if this most
valuable of all fish is to survive.

☐	0 ft
☐	650 ft
☐	3,250 ft
☐	6,500 ft

N

0	Miles	500
0	Kilometers	800

The Aral Sea

Once the world's fourth-largest
lake, the Aral Sea today is a shadow
of its former self. Water from the
two major rivers that feed the lake
is diverted for irrigation and for use
in homes and factories, causing
disastrous consequences for the
local climate and environment.
Between 1960 and 1990, it was
reduced to two-thirds of its original
size. The result is intensely hot
summers with only a fifth of the
rain than fell 50 years earlier. The
fish have disappeared, and scorching
winds drop millions of tons of salt
on surrounding farmland.

Health spa

The Black Sea is a popular destination for
vacationers. Its northern coasts are low, with
sandbars and lagoons, while the southern coasts
are rocky and rise steeply to the towering Pontic
Mountains. People bathe in the hot springs at
Varna in Bulgaria (right), hoping to benefit from
health-giving minerals. Waterspouts are common
on the Black Sea in summer. In the winter there
are severe storms, though the water remains ice-
free and open to shipping from the ports of
Odessa, Sevastopol, and Novorossiysk.

CARIBBEAN SEA & GULF

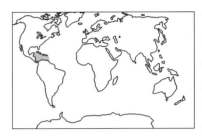

The Caribbean Sea and the Gulf of Mexico, between North and South America, are the western arms of the Atlantic Ocean. They are separated by a curved chain of volcanic islands. The Greater Antilles include Cuba and Jamaica. Hundreds of small islands make up the Bahamas and the Lesser Antilles.

The clear turquoise waters of the Caribbean lap gently at white beaches on islands fringed with palm trees, drawing millions of tourists. More than 5,000 years ago, the earliest inhabitants, the Ciboney and Arawak Native Americans, came to the islands by canoe from South America. From the late 1400s, waves of European settlers claimed the islands as colonies. They set up sugar plantations and brought slaves from Africa to work on them. Along the coast of the Gulf of Mexico are inlets, lagoons, and muddy deltas, including the mouth of the Mississippi. Its silt is rich in minerals, making it a great breeding place for shrimp and other shellfish. It also has important deposits of oil and gas, and thriving shipping and mining industries.

Under the sea

A diver explores the azure sea off the Cayman Islands as a huge reef shark glides overhead. The Caribbean Sea has 75 species of coral as well as parrot fish, flying fish, red snappers and barracuda. It also has five different species of turtle. Conservation groups are currently working to save the rare leatherback turtle from extinction.

Manatee

Manatees live in the warm coastal waters of the Gulf of Mexico, browsing on seagrass that grows in the shallows. They are also called sea cows because of their grazing habits. In the fall, they migrate north to the lagoons and swamps of the Florida Everglades, where they spend the winter feeding on freshwater plants. These gentle creatures have poor eyesight and call to each other to keep in touch. They have no defense against human predators, who hunt them for their meat. Like other types of sea cow, including dugongs, the docile manatees are now endangered.

Panama Canal

The Panama Canal, built by the U.S. and opened in 1914, cuts across the isthmus of Panama from Cristobal on the Atlantic to Balboa on the Pacific. It allows ships to avoid the 7,000-mile (11,300-km) journey around South America. A mere 40 miles (64 km) long, the canal has six pairs of locks and takes eight hours to cross. It was operated jointly by the U.S. and Panama, but was handed over completely to Panama in 2000. One of the world's busiest shipping routes, the Panama Canal transports cargoes of oil, mineral ores, sugar, tobacco, cigars, and tropical hardwoods.

Panama Canal

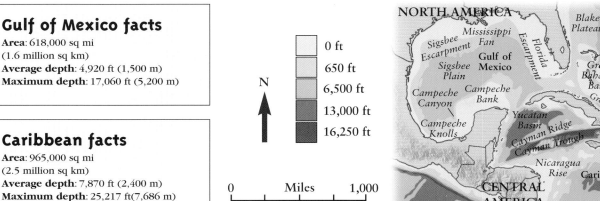

Gulf of Mexico facts

Area: 618,000 sq mi
(1.6 million sq km)
Average depth: 4,920 ft (1,500 m)
Maximum depth: 17,060 ft (5,200 m)

Caribbean facts

Area: 965,000 sq mi
(2.5 million sq km)
Average depth: 7,870 ft (2,400 m)
Maximum depth: 25,217 ft (7,686 m)

Scale:
- 0 ft
- 650 ft
- 6,500 ft
- 13,000 ft
- 16,250 ft

N

| 0 | Miles | 1,000 |
| 0 | Kilometers | 1,600 |

St. Vincent

In the Windward Islands of the Lesser Antilles, the beautiful island of St. Vincent has its own string of islets, the Grenadines. It also has an active volcano, Mt. Soufrière. Several of the plates of Earth's crust meet under the Caribbean at the Puerto Rico Trench. One dives beneath another, creating an arc of volcanic islands. The active volcanoes in the Greater and Lesser Antilles show that islands are still being formed.

Local trader

The white sandy beaches of the Caribbean (left) are made of the limestone shells and skeletons of marine animals. A Caribbean islander (above) holds a conch shell, which she will sell as a souvenir. Behind her in her beach hut are other treasures from the sea, including sea stars. Sadly, tourists who take home these beautiful mementos will be contributing to the depletion of the islands' varied marine life.

Lake Maracaibo

Venezuela's rich reserves of oil are its most important product, and oil exports bring in three-quarters of its income. Most of Venezuela's oil fields are in Lake Maracaibo, which is not really a lake, but a huge inlet from the Caribbean Sea on the northern shores of South America. Lake Maracaibo has abundant wildlife, including large flocks of scarlet ibises, but its waters are threatened with pollution from its many oil installations. The oil is extracted through around 10,000 derricks, and supertankers transport it to refineries on shore. Most tankers are too big to enter port, so they unload at buoy moorings connected to undersea pipelines that lead directly to the oil terminals.

55

PACIFIC OCEAN

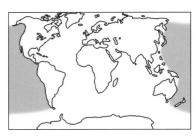

The largest of all the oceans, the Pacific covers one third of the Earth. This ocean holds more water than all the others put together, has the greatest average depth, and plunges in the Marianas Trench to the lowest point on Earth.

The Pacific stretches from the frozen Arctic across the tropics to icy Antarctica, and from Asia and Australia in the west to the Americas in the east. The large islands in the Pacific—such as Japan—have broken away from continents. The thousands of tiny Pacific islands are volcanoes rising from the seabed, many surrounded by coral reefs. Pacific means peaceful, but the ocean rim is a major earthquake and volcano zone. The trade winds that blow across the ocean from northeast and southeast of the equator whip up violent storms called willy-willies in Australia or typhoons (from the Chinese *tai fung*, meaning great wind). When they hit the coast they can snap palm trees and flatten buildings. The Pacific is also the home of the freak current, El Niño, which heats the ocean off Peru and can cause major changes to the climate.

Peoples of the sea

A Pacific islander skims across clear water in an outrigger—a canoe with floats at either side, designed to skim across coral reefs. Pacific islanders are as much at home on water as on land, and rely on the sea for their livelihood. The ocean provides a rich catch of fish, including tuna, flying fish, and all kinds of shellfish.

Ring of fire

Where the Pacific plate collides with its neighbors at the rim of the ocean, the ground shudders and molten rock gushes up, creating most of the world's 1,000 active volcanoes. Called the "Ring of Fire," this troubled zone stretches from New Zealand right around the Pacific to Tierra del Fuego at the tip of South America. It includes a long arc of volcanic islands that runs from Java to Japan. Japan has more than 70 active volcanoes, and hardly a month goes by without an earth tremor.

El Niño wreaks havoc

Every few years, the cold current that flows around the western coast of South America is replaced by the warm El Niño. Scientists don't yet understand exactly why this happens, but its catastrophic effects are felt as far away as Australia on the other side of the Pacific. In 1997-8 Australia was hit by drought. Crops failed in the sizzling heat as the baked earth cracked and rivers dried up, leaving animals to die of thirst.

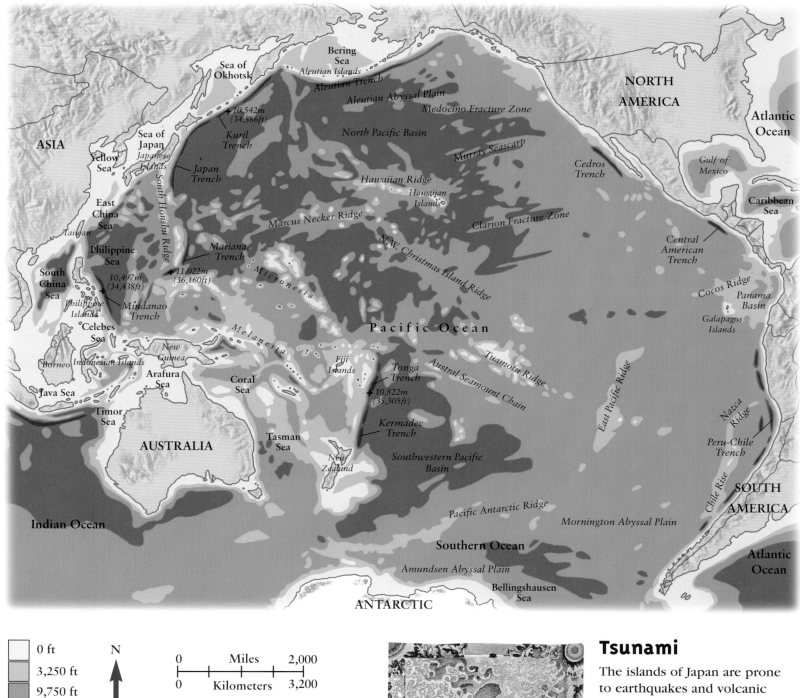

ASIA

NORTH
AMERICA

Atlantic
Ocean

Sea of
Okhotsk

Bering
Sea

Aleutian Islands

Aleutian Trench

Aleutian Abyssal Plain

Medocino Fracture Zone

10,542m
(34,586ft)

Kuril
Trench

Sea of
Japan

Japanese
Islands

North Pacific Basin

Murray Seascarp

Cedros
Trench

Gulf of
Mexico

Yellow
Sea

Japan
Trench

Hawaiian Ridge

Hawaiian
Islands

Clarion Fracture Zone

East
China
Sea

South Honshu Ridge

Marcus Necker Ridge

Caribbean
Sea

Taiwan

Marianas
Trench

Central
American
Trench

Philippine
Sea

11,022m
(36,160ft)

N.W. Christmas Island Ridge

South
China
Sea

10,497m
(34,438ft)

Micronesia

Cocos Ridge

Panama
Basin

Mindanao
Trench

Pacific Ocean

Galapagos
Islands

Philippine
Islands

Celebes
Sea

Melanesia

Fiji
Islands

Tonga
Trench

Tuamotu Ridge

Austral Seamount Chain

Borneo

Indonesian Islands

New
Guinea

10,822m
(35,505ft)

Java Sea

Arafura
Sea

Coral
Sea

Kermadec
Trench

East Pacific Ridge

Nazca
Ridge

Timor
Sea

Tasman
Sea

New
Zealand

Southwestern Pacific
Basin

Peru-Chile
Trench

AUSTRALIA

SOUTH
AMERICA

Indian Ocean

Pacific Antarctic Ridge

Mornington Abyssal Plain

Chile Rise

Atlantic
Ocean

Southern Ocean

Amundsen Abyssal Plain

Bellingshausen
Sea

ANTARCTIC

0 ft
3,250 ft
9,750 ft
16,250 ft
23,000 ft

N

Miles		
0		2,000
0		3,200
Kilometers		

Pacific facts
Area: 64,092,000 sq mi
(166,000,000 sq km)
Average depth: 14,043 ft (4,280 m)
Maximum depth: 36,163 ft
(11,022 m)

Tsunami

The islands of Japan are prone to earthquakes and volcanic eruptions because they are situated on the Pacific Ring of Fire. They also experience tsunami, giant waves generated by earthquakes or volcanoes under the sea. Tsunami is a Japanese word that means "harbor waves." Successive tsunami travel across the ocean at 300 – 370 mph (500 – 600 km/h). The shallows slow them down, and they build up into towering waves that crash onto the coast, causing great loss of life and property. Before each wave there may be a sudden huge withdrawal of water from a bay—the pressure may even suck a harbor dry. Here people sort through their wrecked homes in the wake of tsunami.

PEOPLE AND HISTORY

PACIFIC OCEAN

The history of the Pacific peoples is one of epic migrations across the ocean to settle in lands far from home.

In prehistoric times, hunter-gatherers from Northeast Asia crossed a land bridge from Siberia to Alaska; their descendants became the native peoples of the Americas. The ancestors of Australian Aboriginals crossed a channel that separated prehistoric Australia from Southeast Asia. Southern Chinese sailed across the seas to claim the Pacific Islands. From the 1700s, Europeans ventured into the Pacific. The Europeans established colonies and opened up new trade routes, bringing spices, coconut oil, and sandalwood across the seas.

In the north, Russian traders visited Alaska to buy furs and whaling products. Settlers from Europe set up plantations in the tropics to grow pineapples, sugar cane, and coffee, and brought slaves to work on them. The era of colonialism brought untold hardship. It ended in the 1900s with the independence of the Pacific nations and the rise of their great cities, such as Manila and Singapore.

The world's greatest seafarers

Voyagers sailed from southern China to settle islands in the Polynesian triangle, which covers 8 million sq miles (20 million sq km) of the Pacific. They used canoes, fixed together in pairs with a platform, on which they could sleep and transport food, animals, and plants. The boats were made of reeds, with sails of woven palm leaves. Today's islanders use similar craft to those that brought their ancestors to the islands 5,000 years ago.

Easter Island

Early Polynesian settlers left about 600 huge carved heads and a collection of massive stone houses on Easter Island. The statues, called moai, were sculpted around 1,000 years ago and were believed to have magic powers. Easter Island belongs to Chile, and lies in the Pacific Ocean about 2,000 miles (3,500 km) off its shores. It was so named because it was first reached by Europeans on Easter Sunday, 1722.

Mining guano in the Chincha Islands

The abundant fish stocks in the Pacific off Peru attract fish-eating birds such as cormorants, which nest on rocky coasts and islands including the Chincha Islands. The seabirds' droppings collect on the rocks, and dry. This substance, called guano, is rich in valuable phosphates and is mined to be used in fertilizers. The consequences of guano mining can be severe and leave areas barren and uninhabitable. The mining of guano can also be upset by the occurrence of El Niño, as fish desert the area, the once abundant seabirds disappear and guano is longer formed.

Exxon Valdez disaster

One of the world's worst environmental disasters happened when the *Exxon Valdez* ran aground in Prince William Sound off southern Alaska in 1989, spilling 12 million gallons (45 million liters) of crude oil into the Pacific Ocean. Within a week, the 10-inch (30-cm)-thick layer of oil had spread to cover an area of sea the size of Luxembourg. The slick was washed along by currents, coating rocks and beaches across Alaska's southwest coast, poisoning and suffocating fish, seabirds, and mammals, including sea lions and sea otters. More than 1,000 sea otters and 1 million seabirds died. Alaska had to cancel the opening of herring fisheries in its waters, which meant losing millions of dollars of income. Exxon spent more than a billion dollars employing 11,000 workers on a clean-up campaign.

Valdez

Prince William Sound

Exxon Valdez

Oil slick

Gulf of Alaska

Maoris

Maoris originally came from the Polynesia islands northeast of New Zealand as long ago as the 900s. New Zealand's coastline stretches for more than 4,300 miles (6,900 km) and includes bays, fjords and gulfs that form good natural harbors. Today the Maoris number around 10 percent of the population. Like the Aboriginals of Australia, the Maoris are demanding rights to land taken from them by European settlers in the 1800s.

Papua New Guinea

The history of the people of Papua New Guinea is sketchy, however, evidence suggests there have been people living here for 27,000 years. They live mainly in the thickly forested mountains but also in stilted houses that border swamps, rivers, and estuaries that flood frequently. Today, crocodile farms have sprung up along the coast. These farms produce valuable meat and leather goods.

New Zealand

Lifeguards speed to rescue a surfer in distress off a beach in New Zealand. New Zealand has a high standard of living and a strong reputation for peaceable equality. In 1893, it became the first country in the world to give women the vote. New Zealand bans nuclear-powered and nuclear-armed ships from its waters. In 1985, the Greenpeace trawler *Rainbow Warrior* was protesting against French testing of nuclear bombs in the Pacific when it was blown up in New Zealand waters, killing a photographer aboard. New Zealand forced France to admit responsibility, and demanded compensation in the international courts.

ECONOMY

PACIFIC OCEAN

One of the Pacific's greatest resources is its beauty. Tourists come from all over the world to enjoy white sandy beaches fringed with palms, especially on the island of Bali in Indonesia, at Acapulco in Mexico, and at Honolulu in Hawaii.

Fishing is a major industry, with salmon, cod, and bass being caught over the continental shelves of the North Pacific, and sardines and mackerel around the coasts of the south. Huge supertankers crisscross the ocean, carrying oil and raw materials such as iron ore. Japan and the U.S. are major trading partners, but one third of all the ocean's trade is between countries in the western Pacific. Mining is another source of wealth, both on the coasts and on the continental shelf. Here, molten rock has brought up valuable metals including copper, lead, and silver from deep inside the Earth. In some places, the shelf is covered in phosphates, formed from the remains of dead sea creatures. These are used as fertilizers. In other places, rocks below the continental shelf have trapped huge pockets of oil and gas. In the ocean depths, the seabed is scattered with metal deposits, which could be mined by deep-sea dredges.

Hong Kong

A large wooden junk, the traditional boat of China, sails majestically into Hong Kong harbor against a dramatic background of soaring skyscrapers. Hong Kong is made up of some 236 islands as well as an area on the mainland. It is one of the world's most important ports and financial centers. With six million inhabitants, it is also the planet's third most densely populated city. Many of its people work in industry, manufacturing textiles, clothing, electronic goods, watches, and cameras for export. Hong Kong was a colony of Britain until 1997, when it became part of China.

South Sea tourists

The islands of the South Pacific have acted as a magnet to wealthy tourists who come to the region for the constant sunshine, unspoilt islands and pristine beaches. The pollution-free reefs are a haven for marine life, such as turtles, sharks, and barracuda. This wealth of sea life attracts scuba divers from all corners of the globe. Here they are able to enjoy the crystal clear waters whilst swimming or snorkeling among the underwater caves, coral gardens, and numerous shipwrecks that have foundered here.

Coconuts

Coconut palms wave gently in the breeze along the coasts of tropical islands in the Pacific. The nuts are harvested by agile men and young boys who shinny up the trees to cut them. Coconuts are very important in the Pacific diet. They yield a refreshing milky drink, which can be enjoyed straight from the nut. The delicious flesh can be eaten raw or used in sweet and savoury cooking. Desiccated (dried) coconut is a valuable export, as is coconut oil, used to make margarine and soap. The tough fibers on the coconut shell can be woven into mats or used in garden compost.

Tuna fishing

Tuna fishing is an important industry in the Pacific, as the fish are canned for export and sold fresh all over the world. Traditionally, tuna are caught far out in the open sea on a line that may be as long as 110 miles (180 km), trailed behind a fishing boat. As many as 200 short lines branch off the main line, each armed with a baited hook. When the tuna bites, it takes several men to haul the giant fish aboard and kill it with spears. More commonly today, tuna fishers use enormous drift nets, which accidentally kill dolphins, turtles, and other creatures as well as catching tuna. Following protests by environmentalists, cans of tuna not caught in drift nets are labelled "dolphin-friendly."

Fish farming

In Ecuador (below), coastal mangrove swamps have been cleared to make way for shrimp farms. These carefully managed farms produce good quality shrimp that are exported all over the world. Off the shores of Japan, yellowtail fish, and bluefin tuna are raised in cages under the sea. Farming fish is more cost-effective than catching them—a farmed bluefin tuna will increase in weight by 300 times over just four years.

Giant spider crab

The Japanese giant spider crab is the world's largest crustacean—and a great delicacy in Japan. Its body can be more than 12 inches (30 cm) in diameter and it can measure as much as 11 $\frac{1}{2}$ feet (3.5 m) across from claw to claw. This huge crab camouflages itself by planting a garden on its back. With its strong pincers, it cuts seaweed and sponges from the rocks, roughens them up with its mouthparts, then attaches them to its shell and legs, which are covered with tiny hooks. During the day the crab rests motionless on the seabed, unnoticed under its ingenious disguise.

NORTH PACIFIC SHORES

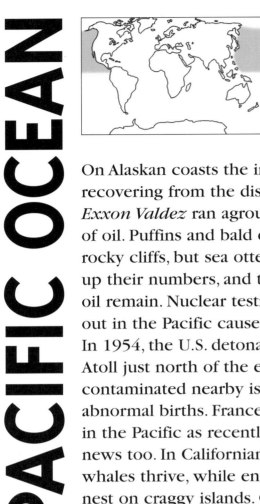

In the far North Pacific the Inuit people of the Aleutian Islands hunt fish, seals, and whales, using every scrap of what they catch.

On Alaskan coasts the injured ecosystem is slowly recovering from the disaster of 1989, when the *Exxon Valdez* ran aground and spilled its vast cargo of oil. Puffins and bald eagles make their nests on rocky cliffs, but sea otters are still struggling to build up their numbers, and toxic lumps and pockets of oil remain. Nuclear testing on tiny coral islands far out in the Pacific causes a different kind of damage. In 1954, the U.S. detonated a nuclear bomb on Bikini Atoll just north of the equator. Radioactive fallout contaminated nearby islands, causing cancer and abnormal births. France carried out nuclear testing in the Pacific as recently as 1996. Yet there is good news too. In Californian marine sanctuaries, blue whales thrive, while endangered brown pelicans nest on craggy islands. California sea lions have become so abundant in Monterey Bay that they steal salmon from anglers' lines.

Tea clipper

The strange name "clipper" comes from this ship's speed and its ability to cut, or clip, the time of its journey. Tea clippers were built in Britain at the beginning of the 1800s for the tea trade with China. It was traditional for clippers to race home with the new crop of tea. The greatest race ever was in 1866, when five ships docked within two hours—the prize money was shared between all of them—and the price of tea fell because there was so much of it.

World War II in the Pacific

A fleet of Japanese aircraft carriers waits 300 miles (500 km) out in the Pacific off Tokyo in March 1945, expecting an Allied attack. The deck in the foreground bristles with the folded wings of fighter planes. Japan attacked the U.S. Pacific Fleet at Pearl Harbor in 1941, quickly overran Hong Kong, Singapore, and the Philippines, and advanced to India and Australia. From 1942 the U.S. waged a devastatingly successful campaign against the Japanese, eventually forcing the Japanese back to their home islands. When Japan refused to surrender, the first atomic bomb was dropped on Hiroshima in August 1945. After a second bomb fell on Nagasaki three days later, Japan conceded defeat.

Kamchatka

In the far northwestern Pacific, the mountainous Russian peninsula of Kamchatka divides the Sea of Okhotsk from the Bering Sea. Kamchatka is famed for its geysers—springs that throw up steam and hot water, heated by molten rock deep under Earth's crust. Kamchatka is the breeding ground of Steller's sea eagle, a magnificent fish-eating bird that measures 10 feet (3 m) from wing tip to wing tip. Named after Georg Steller, the German naturalist who explored Kamchatka in the 1700s, the eagles fly south to Japan to escape the worst of the Russian winter.

Californian beach

Californians are known for their zeal for health and fitness. Many coast-dwellers exercise on the long sandy beaches of the "Golden State." Surfing, hang gliding, and windsurfing are all popular pastimes in California. Great white sharks cruise the waters off Catalina and Monterey. Whales also migrate along this coast and whale watching boats are commonplace.

Shanghai, China

The bustling Pacific port of Shanghai, built on the mouths of two great rivers, is the largest city in China. It is the most heavily populated area in the world, with an average of 7 sq yards (6 sq m) of living space per person. Shanghai rose to prominence in the 1800s when it became an important center of foreign trade. Today, Shanghai handles about half of all China's imports and exports. Its industries include steel and oil refining.

Seaweed

Seaweed is harvested in the waters off Japan (above). It is widely farmed in Japanese waters, for it is highly nutritious and considered a delicacy, either deep-fried or wrapped around raw fish to make sushi. Once harvested, seaweed is hung in the air to dry. Extracts of seaweed are used in the manufacture of ice cream and toothpaste. But seaweed is also an important source of food for many marine creatures, and extensive harvesting disrupts the food chain.

Alaskan wilderness

One of Alaska's islands lies barely 2 1/2 miles (4 km) from a Russian island across the Bering Strait. Alaska once belonged to Russia, but was sold to the U.S. for just 7 million dollars in 1867. In 1880, gold was discovered there. Its economy thrives on mines, forests, and salmon fisheries. The exploitation of vast deposits of oil threatens fragile Arctic habitats. The climate of Alaska has warmed considerably and glaciers are retreating. Study of the Alaskan wilderness may hold clues to global climate change.

PACIFIC ISLANDS

PACIFIC OCEAN

Besides the large islands of Japan, the Philippines, New Guinea, and New Zealand, there are thousands of tiny islands scattered across the Pacific Ocean. They are home to about five million islanders, who share one great common resource: the sea.

Some islands are mountainous; others are coral atolls. Most are clustered in the southwestern Pacific, though some, such as Easter Island and Hawaii, are isolated thousands of miles from their neighbors. The islands grow cocoa, coffee, vanilla beans, and bananas for export. Mines produce gold and phosphates for the fertilizer industry. Coconuts are processed to make palm oil, and tourism is increasing. Most islanders make their living by fishing, but not always by traditional methods.

Off Papua New Guinea in the tropical western Pacific, enormous bump-head parrot fish bite the corals, ingesting them for algae. But there are dangers in this underwater paradise. Illegal blast fishing, with explosions caused by a lethal mixture of fertilizer and diesel oil, is destroying the reefs. Another illegal practice is pouring cyanide into the waters. This stuns fish, which are then collected for the world's growing aquarium industry as well as for food. Poisoned fish are on sale throughout Southeast Asia, in cities such as Manila and Singapore.

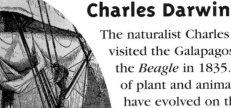

Charles Darwin

The naturalist Charles Darwin visited the Galapagos aboard the *Beagle* in 1835. Hundreds of plant and animal species have evolved on the islands in isolation from mainland species. About half the birds and insects, one-third of the plants, and 90 percent of the other animals exist nowhere else on Earth. His study of this extraordinary ecosystem led Darwin to develop his theory of evolution in 1859.

Nesting turtles

Green turtles drag themselves beyond the high-tide mark and excavate a hole with their rear flippers. They lay around 100 eggs and then cover them in sand. The eggs hatch in 50 to 60 days, then the hatchlings dig their way out of the sand and struggle down to the comparative safety of the sea.

Kilauea erupts

The Hawaiian Islands lie in the middle of the Pacific and are not part of the Ring of Fire. They are hot spot volcanoes, which form where molten rock burns through the Earth's crust. Two of the world's biggest volcanoes, Mauna Loa and Kilauea (left), erupt almost constantly, spewing forth plumes of fire. A new island, Loihi, is forming under the sea.

Hub of the Pacific

Hawaii's 20 palm-fringed islands form a growing string of volcanoes. The sunny climate remains virtually unchanged all year, ripening crops of coffee and attracting tourists. They come to ride the surf at Honolulu or to visit the site of Pearl Harbor, the scene of the Japanese attack in 1941 that brought the U.S. into World War II. They also visit the humpback whale sanctuary. Nearly two-thirds of the estimated 8,000 North Pacific humpback whales mate and calve here, their only U.S. breeding ground.

Tasmania

Wind and waves have worn away this soft sandstone beach in Tasmania to create an unusual rock formation called a tessellated (tiled) pavement. The rock pools left by the tide are rich with seaweed, small fish, and crustaceans. The mountainous island of Tasmania lies 155 miles (250 km) off Southeast Australia. It enjoys a mild climate, with plenty of rainfall blowing in off the sea.

Fijian glory

Morning glory blooms in the sand, stabilizing the beaches of Fiji—a group of 800 islands of which only 80 are inhabited. Forests cover the islands' volcanic slopes. The economy relies on crops of sugar, cocoa, coconuts, and ginger, and on the tourists who come to visit coral reefs and beaches. Europeans began visiting the islands in search of sandalwood. The islands later became important as a provisions base for whalers.

Mussel farming

The green-lipped mussel is found only in the waters off New Zealand. This delicacy has become a valuable export, and mussels are now farmed off the coast. Mussels are bivalves. They produce tough threads that anchor them in place, and filter food from the water as the tide or currents wash over them. They often cluster together on underwater structures such as seawalls, and in mussel farms they are encouraged to grow up a framework for easy harvesting. The green-lipped mussel also produces an extract that is used in the treatment of arthritis.

SOUTH PACIFIC SHORES

PACIFIC OCEAN

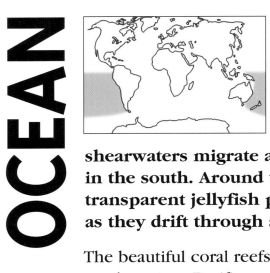

The rich wildlife of the South Pacific includes sea snakes, turtles, and dolphins. Cormorants and boobies nest on rocky crags and fish off the coast of Peru. Gray whales and slender-billed fish-eating shearwaters migrate across vast distances to overwinter in the south. Around the tropics, transparent jellyfish pulse gently as they drift through azure lagoons.

The beautiful coral reefs of the southwestern Pacific are at risk from pollution and overfishing. Tourism also damages the reefs, and traders trap the brightly colored fish that live there to sell to the worldwide aquarium trade, disrupting the food chain. The sad degradation of coral reefs has serious consequences for people as well as for wildlife. Reef fish make up 10 percent of the global fish catch, and are an important source of income and nourishment for the people of the tropical shorelines. Reefs also act as buffers against coastal erosion and storm surges.

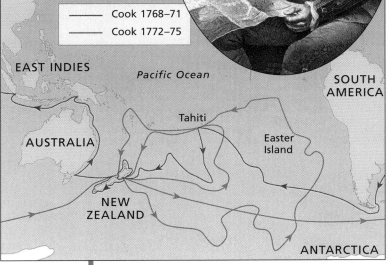

——	Cook 1768–71
——	Cook 1772–75

EAST INDIES · Pacific Ocean · SOUTH AMERICA · Tahiti · Easter Island · AUSTRALIA · NEW ZEALAND · ANTARCTICA

The voyages of Captain Cook

Europe's greatest Pacific explorer was the Englishman Captain James Cook. He led three major expeditions between 1768 and 1779. During the first, he mapped New Zealand and explored the strait that separates its two islands. On the second, he surveyed the entire coast of Australia. In an attempt to find out whether another great continent lay in the Pacific, he also visited Easter Island, the Marquesas, Tonga, Tahiti, and Vanuatu, and discovered New Caledonia, Norfolk Island, and the Isle of Pines. On his third voyage, he found Hawaii and explored the coast of North America. After sailing south along the coast of Asia, he returned to Hawaii, where he was killed by local people.

Shark fishing

A catch of sharks awaits refrigeration in Sydney harbor. Shark is a popular dish in Australia, and the fish is also valued for its skin, which is used as leather. But the exploitation of sharks has reduced their numbers, and some species are now protected. These include the great white, the tiger shark, and the hammerhead.

Convict ships

Three ships leave London for Australia in 1862. On board are convicts being deported. Some were not criminals, but "undesirables," such as the "Tolpuddle Martyrs." These six Dorset farm workers were sentenced to transportation in 1834 for swearing an oath of loyalty to the laborers' union in the village of Tolpuddle. Transportation began in 1788 and went on for 80 years. During that time some 1,040 convict ships delivered more than 160,000 prisoners to Australia, where they helped establish a new British colony.

Fishing in Peru

Fishermen mend their nets on a beach in Peru. In the background are their boats, traditional canoes made of reeds. Their high prows make for a fast passage across the waves as the men paddle out to sea in search of anchovies. On the right is another form of fishing boat, a simple raft. The waters off Peru are a rich fishing ground, but in an El Niño year, when the warm current drives the anchovies into deeper waters, the fishermen have to find another way of making a living.

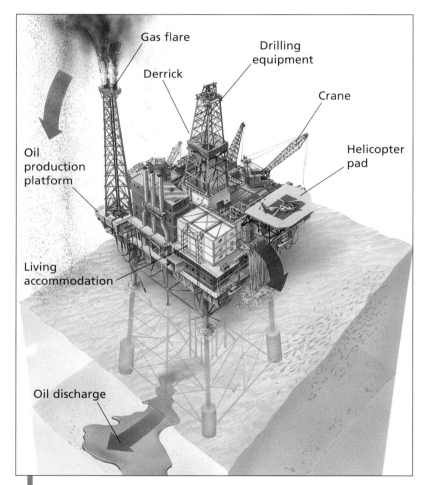

Drilling for oil off Australia

The legs of this semi-submersible oil platform are filled with water to hold the rig down on the seabed. A metal derrick on the platform lowers and raises the drilling equipment. As the drill bit cuts through rock in search of oil below the seabed, oily mud is pumped down the drill shaft to lubricate the bit and help stop oil leaks from the shaft. Later, this mud is dumped in the sea. Some of the oil is removed first, but serious pollution is caused by this deliberate dumping. When oil is extracted from the mixture pumped out of the seabed, the oily water left behind is also discharged into the sea.

Salt ponds

In Vietnam, salt is produced by a labor-intensive method. These two women, wrapped up in masks, straw hats, and gloves to protect their skin from the Sun, sit on a wooden framework and operate paddles with their feet. The paddles push salt water from the South China Sea into shallow ponds. There it will evaporate in the fierce heat, leaving behind a thick deposit of salt, which can be shovelled into heaps and carted away. The Vietnamese government plans to increase its salt production so the country can begin to export it.

The Strait of Magellan

The port of Punta Arenas lies on the Strait of Magellan. The Portuguese navigator Ferdinand Magellan was the first European to cross through this strait located at the tip of South America in 1520. Magellan would have been the first person to sail around the world, but he was killed by islanders in the Philippines. His ship went on to complete the voyage commanded by Sebastian del Cano.

GREAT BARRIER REEF

PACIFIC OCEAN

Stretching 1,250 miles (2,000 km) along the eastern coast of Australia, the Great Barrier Reef is one of the world's most beautiful habitats. In its azure blue waters, rainbow colored fish dart among corals of all colors and shapes. Corals are not plants, they are colonies of tiny animals called polyps.

Each coral polyp secretes a chalky material that forms a protective tube around its body. As it grows, younger polyps bud off it, and so a colony is formed. Each generation builds on top of the last, and the colony grows. Many colonies make up a reef. The reef teems with millions of fish that feed on the algae growing on the coral. It also provides shelter for a huge variety of marine animals, such as sea turtles, giant clams, sea cucumbers, and seahorses. Manta rays drift across the reef and nurse sharks cruise at its fringes. The worst threat to the reef is from humans. Another enemy is the crown of thorns sea star—one of these creatures can eat 6 square yards (5 sq m) of coral in one year.

Moray eel

A hunter that feeds on squid and fish, the moray eel lurks in a dark crevice waiting for its prey to swim past, then seizes it in its powerful jaws, which it also uses to bite its enemies. There are about 100 types of moray eel and many are brightly patterned to camouflage them against the colorful reef.

Lionfish

The lionfish has many other names, including scorpion fish and firefish, and is one of the most poisonous of all sea creatures. Glands of deadly venom lie at the base of the spines on its back, under its head, and below its tail. It warns off potential predators with its bright stripes. Sighting prey, it darts forward to strike. It can paralyze any predator and even kill a human.

Cleaner wrasse

The small blue fish by the huge mouth of the coral trout is a cleaner wrasse. Cleaners eat parasites such as fish lice off the skin of other fish, and often work inside the mouths of large predators. The cleaner's vivid stripes and darting swimming pattern help draw it to the attention of bigger fish, which often line up with their mouths and gill covers open, waiting for its services.

Nautilus

Unlike its relatives, the squid and octopus, the nautilus cannot squirt ink to hide from its enemies. Instead, it lives in a shiny protective shell. Inside, the shell is divided into about 30 compartments. The nautilus lives in the first and largest— the others are buoyancy chambers filled with gas. The nautilus drifts along, stretching out its tentacles to catch prey.

Parrot fish

The parrot fish is named for its beak-shaped mouth, which is adapted for biting off coral tips. It grinds them with its platelike teeth, digests the algae growing on the coral, then excretes the coral as fine sand, which builds up in the shallow-water area.

INDIAN OCEAN

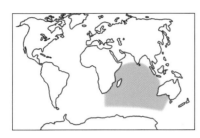

The Indian Ocean is the world's third largest ocean. Bordered by Africa, Asia, and Australia, it straddles the equator and stretches south to the icy waters of the Antarctic. It includes the Arabian Sea and the Bay of Bengal and its arms extend into the Red Sea and the Arabian Gulf.

The Indian Ocean has a few large islands, including Madagascar and Sumatra, and many tiny volcanic islands fringed with coral, as well as atolls and shallow lagoons. The ocean floor is divided by deep canyons and mountain ridges. Scattered across it are huge seamounts and small volcanic hills. Below the equator the West Australian Current moves cold Antarctic waters counterclockwise. Currents in the North Indian Ocean follow seasonal monsoon-bearing winds, flowing clockwise in the summer and counterclockwise in winter. These changing currents helped seafarers of the past to make long return voyages across the ocean. The torrential monsoon rains that lash the coasts enable valuable food and rubber crops to be grown in places such as Malaysia, but bring flooding and devastation elsewhere, as do seasonal cyclones and occasional tsunami.

The Maldives

A string of 1,200 tiny tropical islands called the Maldives lies in the turquoise waters south of India. Only 200 of them are inhabited, and many are atolls, which are coral reefs surrounding a lagoon. All are low-lying and may eventually be completely submerged as the sea level rises due to global warming. The people of the Maldives live mainly by fishing and tourism. They also grow pineapples, pomegranates, and yams, but have to import staples such as rice.

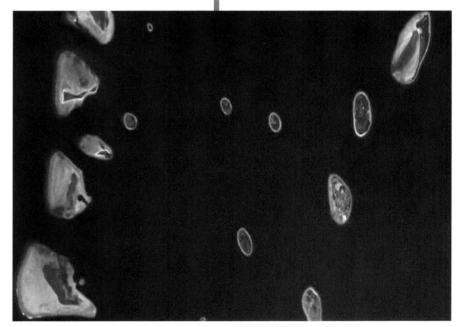

Extinct

The dodo was unique to the island of Mauritius, which lies to the east of Madagascar in the Indian Ocean. Related to the pigeon, but larger than a turkey, it became extinct in the 1600s. The dodo was flightless and trusting, making easy prey for humans, who clubbed the bird to death for food. It was also hunted by the animals that sailors introduced from other lands. Dodo means "sleepy" or "stupid" in French. The last surviving flightless bird of the Indian Ocean, the white-throated rail, is being studied by naturalists in its habitat on the atoll of Aldabra in the Seychelles.

Wildlife of Madagascar

The large island of Madagascar separated from the African mainland about 160 mya, and many of its animals evolved into species seen nowhere else on Earth. Ring-tailed lemurs are unique to the island. They are active during the day, moving on the ground and in the trees where they feed on fruit, leaves, and bark. The females lead the troops. The males claim territory with stink battles using scent from a gland under the tail. Lemurs are under threat from the depletion of their forest habitat. They are also often shot by the locals as pests.

Fruit of the sea

The coco-de-mer is the nut of a palm tree that grows in the Seychelles, a group of islands lying 750 miles (1,200 km) off the coast of East Africa. At 20 inches (50 cm) long, this rare nut is the world's largest seed, and protected by the Seychelles government. Those that fall into the sea and get borne away can travel thousands of miles before washing up on distant shores. All around the Indian Ocean, the seed was prized by the people who found it, who believed it to have magical and medicinal properties.

Pirates

Operating from islands in Indonesia, pirates scour the seas for bounty. Wearing masks to hide their identities, the pirates leave their haunt at dusk and zoom across the ocean in an unmarked speedboat. When they find a likely vessel, they clamber on board with the aid of grappling hooks and rope ladders to rob the crew or passengers at knifepoint. Some gangs have been known to ambush and steal whole oil tankers with the help of corrupt officials.

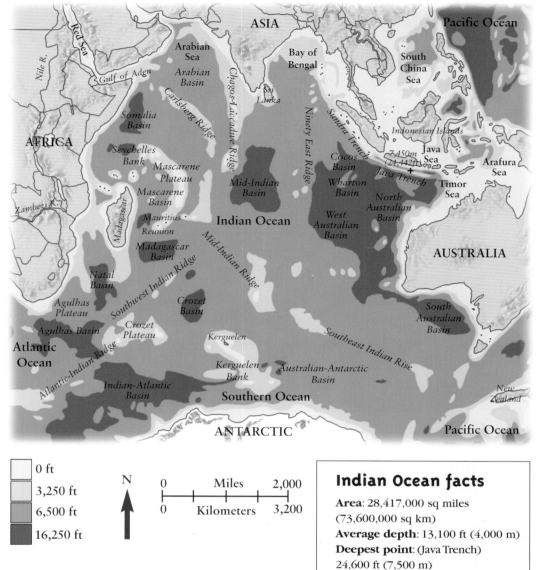

0 ft	
3,250 ft	
6,500 ft	
16,250 ft	

N

Miles		2,000
0		
0	Kilometers	3,200

Indian Ocean facts

Area: 28,417,000 sq miles (73,600,000 sq km)
Average depth: 13,100 ft (4,000 m)
Deepest point: (Java Trench) 24,600 ft (7,500 m)

Flooding in Bangladesh

Bangladesh on the Bay of Bengal is a low-lying country threaded with rivers that flow to join the huge Ganges delta, the largest delta in the world. When the torrential monsoon rains come, the rivers burst their banks. Over the years millions of people have been drowned or made homeless, livestock has been lost, and crops have washed away, causing famine. Flooding is sometimes followed by epidemics of disease, and the plight of the people is often made worse by the cyclones that regularly hit the shores.

PEOPLE AND HISTORY

INDIAN OCEAN

The ancient Egyptians, Phoenicians, Persians, and Indians were the first seafarers to sail the Indian Ocean, searching for new lands with which to trade. Their wooden ships crisscrossed the seas, carrying spices, ivory, and bales of cloth.

In the 1400s, the great Chinese explorer Cheng Ho led his ships westwards to Sri Lanka, Persia, Arabia, and Africa. Coming from the opposite direction, the Portuguese navigator Vasco da Gama opened up trade routes from Europe. He was followed by fleets from Britain, France, and The Netherlands. The Europeans occupied important ports and set up colonies along their trading routes. Tea clippers raced around the stormy Cape of Good Hope at the southern tip of Africa, giving the Trade Winds and the Trade Wind Currents their names. Pirates roamed the seas, making their haunts on islands such as the Seychelles. Seafarers killed many of the islands' unique animals for meat—the giant tortoises of Rodrigues were extinct by 1800. Today many islanders make their living through fishing and tourism. Fruit and flowers are grown on tropical islands for export to the U.S. and Europe.

Henry the Navigator

Portugal's Prince Henry the Navigator (1394-1460) was not a navigator. He was given this honorary title because he set up a school for navigators, and financed expeditions along the west coast of Africa. He called on the best geographers of Europe to help plan his voyages and train captains and pilots in astronomy and cartography (mapmaking). Henry also built an observatory to teach navigation by the stars. His work inspired Portuguese explorers to sail around the Cape of Good Hope and find a route to India and the Far East.

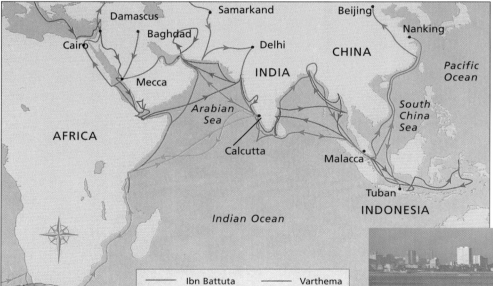

Vasco da Gama

The first European to sail around the Cape of Good Hope was Bartholomew Dias in 1488. Terrible storms and the crew's fear of that they had reached the end of the world drove him back. In 1497, Vasco da Gama, sailed around the Cape, up the coast of East Africa, and across to Calcutta in India. He returned home with a cargo of valuable spices.

Mumbai

The British set up the East India Trading Company in the port of Bombay in 1685, employing women there to make cotton cloth for export. Today Bombay is called Mumbai, and is a major industrial and engineering center. Local people enjoy a stroll along the waterfront to buy coconuts, fruit, and snacks.

Island fisheries

A man sorts fish in the early morning light after landing his catch in Male, the capital of the Maldives. Local fishermen supply the 55,000 inhabitants plus the large numbers of tourists who come to visit these beautiful coral islands. The first settlers here were Buddhists who sailed across the Indian Ocean from Sri Lanka around 500 A.D. Their modern-day descendants speak Dhiveli, a language that gave the world the word "atoll." From the 1300s, traders from China visited the Maldives. They brought with them Ming vases, fragments of which can still sometimes be found on the islands' beaches.

Mining

Zircon (below) is just one of the minerals mined from beach sands in the state of Kerala in southern India. This very hard-wearing mineral is used in industry, though when yellow or transparent deposits are found, they are prized as gemstones. Cassiterite, a major source of tin, is mined around Myanmar (Burma), Thailand, and Indonesia. It was one of the first minerals to be extracted from under the sea. Enormous dredgers, looking more like floating factories than ships, scoop up sediment from the seabed in shallow waters and transfer it to plants on land, where the tin is extracted.

Diving to see corals

The attraction of diving to see the beautiful underwater world of the coral reefs draws huge numbers of tourists to the Indian Ocean, but sadly, they cause damage to the reefs by collecting or buying coral from local traders and polluting the sea with sewage. Humans are not the only threat to corals. In the Red Sea, which has over 350 species of coral—the greatest diversity of any waters in the world—a surge of overheated water killed an area of coral and bleached it white (above). Corals get their vibrant colors from the algae living on them, and these need exactly the right conditions to survive.

Naval bases

The Indian Ocean islands of the Maldives, Seychelles, Comoros, and Diego Garcia make attractive military bases for powerful countries. The United States, Russia, and China have a strategic interest in the Indian Ocean because it commands the important Straits of Hormuz and Bab el Mandeb, which lead to the Middle East, and the Straits of Malacca and Lombok, which lead to the South China Sea.

EASTERN SHORES

INDIAN OCEAN

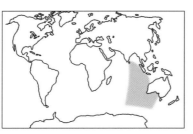

Golden beaches, muddy estuaries, and steaming swamps fringe the coasts of the eastern Indian Ocean.

In the Bay of Bengal, herons and gavials thrive in the muddy waters of the great Ganges estuary. Every year in the monsoon rains, the Ganges bursts its many banks, causing widespread flooding. Many Indonesian coasts are fringed with mangroves. These trees are often called the nurseries of the sea because their spreading roots provide an ideal breeding ground for fish. The Indonesian islands divide the Indian Ocean from the waters of the Pacific. They are part of the active volcano chain that forms the Ring of Fire. Despite frequent volcanic eruptions, people still live near the smoldering volcanoes because their ash makes the soil rich and fertile.

Jute harvest

Workers commute by boat to harvest a tall, whiplike plant called jute that thrives in the muddy riverbeds of the many-mouthed Ganges delta. Its stems are cut and tied in sheaves to dry in the Sun. Tough jute fibers are used to make rope, sacking, and matting. Jute was also used for webbing in upholstery and on the backs of tufted-pile carpets, until it was replaced with synthetic materials. Bangladesh grows the best quality jute in the world, and it is the country's most important export.

Harvesting the sea

Many Indian Ocean communities have devised ways of fishing without going out to sea. Here a stilt fisherman perches precariously above a surging tide on a Sri Lankan beach. He fishes with a rod and line, and stores his catch in nets that hang beside him. On the Indian coast, wooden jetties of logs lashed together with rope are built out into the sea. Scoop nets suspended from tall poles are erected at the end of these jetties to catch the fish left behind when the tide goes out.

Great white shark

The world's largest predatory shark is the great white, feared in all the warmer waters of the world. It can grow to 20 feet (6 m) in length, and its huge jaws contain rapier-sharp teeth that grow up to $2^1/2$ inches (6 cm) long. The great white hunts squid, tuna, and turtles, as well as seals, dolphins, and other sharks. It can also attack people, mistaking them for dolphins, though humans have killed far more great whites than great whites have killed humans. So many great whites have been slaughtered by hunters that this shark is now endangered, and has become a protected species in many parts of the world.

Krakatoa

Krakatoa blows its top (below). The volcanic island of Krakatoa is uninhabited. It lies between Java and Sumatra in Indonesia, and was devastated in1883 by a huge eruption. The massive shock triggered huge tsunami that rolled across the ocean and crashed onto Java and Sumatra, causing 36,000 deaths.

Gavial

A crocodilian called a gavial lives in the muddy waters of the Ganges delta in Bangladesh. It spends more time in the water than it does on land, and its webbed hind feet make it a powerful swimmer. The gavial feeds mainly on fish, and its long, narrow snout and jagged teeth are well adapted for catching them. It lurks in the shallows waiting for a shoal to swim by, then chases it, swinging its jaws sideways into the darting fish and snapping them up. The gavial reproduces by laying up to 40 eggs in a nest on the riverbank.

Phuket

Strange rocky outcrops, like this one off Phuket Island, rise steeply out of the emerald sea around the coast of Thailand. Most of the 40 rocky islands in Phang Nga Bay are uninhabited. Many of the islands have spectacular collapsed cave systems that are open to the sky. These "rooms" surrounded by towering limestone walls, are hidden realms rich in unspoiled wildlife.

Floating market

Bamboo is the fastest-growing plant in the world—the giant bamboo can grow up to 18 inches (46 cm) a day. It is a native of Myanmar (Burma), and its stems are used for making buckets, chopsticks—and boats. On this river many boats and rafts made of bamboo have come together for a floating market. Sometimes several rafts are lashed together to make a raft large enough for many different traders to sell their wares. Customers arrive and take their goods away by boat. Bamboo rafts and boats are also used for sea travel near the coast.

RED SEA & PERSIAN GULF

INDIAN OCEAN

Like two fingers pointing up from the Indian Ocean, the Red Sea and the Persian Gulf stretch northward at either side of the Arabian Peninsula. These deep blue expanses of water sparkle under the fierce Sun, providing a dramatic contrast with the barren deserts along their shores.

The Arab lands around these two seas are sparsely populated, though new ports and big cities have sprung up there since the discovery of oil. Huge reserves of oil have made countries that were once very poor among the richest nations in the world.

The Red Sea gets its name from the red patches of phytoplankton that sometimes float on its surface. They form the base of the sea's food chain, feeding fish and some of the longest stretches of unspoilt corals in the world. Hot, salty water wells up from clefts on the seabed, caused by molten rock under the Earth's surface where the plates are pushing apart.

The Persian Gulf is one of the hottest, driest parts of the world, and has more than half the world's total reserves of oil. The waters of the Gulf are shallow and calm, which makes drilling easier. The legs of the rig are drilled into the seabed and the oil is transported by pipeline to refineries onshore, or by supertanker to distant ports.

Spice boats

Arabian boats called dhows sailed the Indian Ocean over 1,300 years ago. Dhows were the first boats to use a lateen, a triangular sail. This was a vast improvement on square-rigged sails, which made craft very difficult to sail against the wind. Dhows enabled Arab traders to cross to India, Southeast Asia, and China, carrying cargoes of spices, silks, and jewels. Their voyages helped spread the culture and ideas of Islam, the religion of the Arab world.

The Afar Triangle

The Red Sea lies on a rift between Africa and Arabia, where the Earth's plates are pushing the continents apart. The Afar Triangle is a flat triangle of land at the southern end of the Red Sea in Djibouti. It was once covered by the sea, but the movement of the Earth's crust has lifted it up above sea level. In this inhospitable desert are thick deposits of sea salt, formed by salt water that evaporated. There are also strange ash rings—the remains of underwater volcanic eruptions.

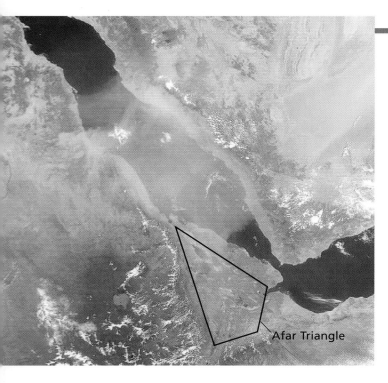

Afar Triangle

Clear waters

A liner cruises down the Red Sea toward the Gulf of Aden. The shallow turquoise waters teem with life. There are reefs of delicate coral and beds of seagrass where dugongs graze. Highly salt-tolerant mangrove trees grow in some inlets, and fish and shellfish shelter and feed among their spreading roots.

The Gulf War

The economy of Iraq, which lies at the top of the Persian Gulf, is built on its vast oil reserves, which are especially rich in the south. In 1990, Iraq invaded Kuwait, across its southern border. The following year, troops from 28 nations, including Britain and the U.S., drove back the Iraqis. Iraq retaliated by bombing hundreds of Kuwaiti oil wells. Fierce fires filled the desert air with toxic black smoke, as oil burned unchecked. The land and sea were severely polluted, and Kuwait's economy was badly damaged. After the war ended, a multinational effort was made toward restoring the blasted Kuwaiti environment.

Red Sea facts

Area: 169,100 sq miles (438,000 sq km)
Length: 1,197 miles (1,930 km)
Maximum width: 190 miles (306 km)
Maximum depth: 9,580 ft (2,920 m)

0 ft	
650 ft	
3,250 ft	
6,500 ft	
9,800 ft	
13,000 ft	

Miles — 0 to 1,000
Kilometers — 0 to 1,600

N

Pearl

Persian Gulf facts

Area: 93,000 sq miles (241,000 sq km)
Length: 613 miles (989 km)
Width: 34 to 210 miles (55 to 340 km)
Depth: less than 295 ft (90 m)

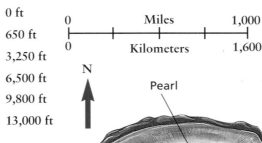

Pearl farming

Off the Gulf island of Bahrain, men dive from a dhow, a traditional Arab craft. They will bring up oysters, hoping to find pearls inside. This region was well known for its pearls even in Roman times, when they formed a valuable export for Arab traders visiting India and China. Thousands of oysters have to be collected in order to harvest a handful of pearls, which makes them extremely precious. Today, cultured (farmed) pearls are much more common. The commercial cultivation of pearls was first carried out by a Japanese noodle salesman. The Frenchman who devised the technique could find no one interested in giving him financial backing for the process.

Fresh water from the sea

At a desalination plant, salt is removed from sea water to produce fresh water that can be used in homes, in industry, and to irrigate farmland. Water is held in storage towers because large-scale evaporation in the scorching heat would make reservoirs useless. Desalination is expensive and uses a great deal of fuel, but this is no problem in the oil-rich Gulf. Many countries such as Bahrain, Qatar, and the United Arab Emirates rely totally on desalination because they are desert lands that have no supplies of fresh water at all. Up until a century ago, Kuwait had to import its drinking water by boat.

GLOSSARY

algae Simple plants, most of which live in water.

archipelago Group of islands.

atoll Coral reef surrounding a lagoon.

baleen Fringed plates that hang from the roof of the mouth of the largest whales and filter their food.

brackish Slightly salty.

colonial animals Animals that live in groups of interconnected and closely related individuals.

colony A territory occupied by settlers from another state, which rules the territory from afar.

continental shelf The rim of a continental landmass.

continental slope The slope on the seaward side of the continental shelf down to a depth of around 9,750 ft (3,000 m).

coral Small marine polyps related to sea anemones, which produce protective outer casings. Over centuries these casings build up to form coral reefs.

current A body of water flowing through the sea like a river. Winds drive surface currents. Deep-sea currents occur where dense cold water sinks and moves across the seabed.

delta Mouths of a river that spread out across a plain to enter the sea.

desalinate To remove salt from water.

earthquake Violent shaking of the earth caused when two continental plates (parts of the Earth's crust) collide or scrape past each other.

erosion Wearing away by wind, rain, or waves.

estuary The mouth of a river where it enters the sea.

eutrophication When pollution causes water to be over-rich in organic or mineral nutrients. Algae then grow on the nutrients in the water, depleting its oxygen supply and killing fish.

evolution The gradual change in characteristics of a population of animals or plants over generations.

food chain Food pathway linking different species in an ecosystem. Energy flows along a food chain from plants to plant eaters, to meat eaters.

fjord A steep-sided coastal inlet formed by a glacier.

fossil fuel Fuels including coal, oil, and gas, produced from the decay, burial, and fossilization of plant and animal remains.

generator A device that produces electricity.

geology The study of the structure and origins of the Earth.

glacier A river of ice that builds up in a mountain valley with the compression of snow.

global warming The warming of Earth's climate caused by an increase in "greenhouse gases" such as carbon dioxide in the atmosphere.

gyre A great loop formed by surface currents circling the ocean.

hurricane A tropical storm with high-speed winds. Also called cyclone or typhoon.

hydroelectricity Electricity derived from falling or moving water.

irrigation A system that brings water to dry land so that crops may grow there.

isthmus A narrow stretch of land joining two wider landmasses.

kelp A long, fast-growing seaweed that provides food and shelter for many marine creatures.

lagoon A body of water cut off from the open sea by coral reefs or sandbars.

land bridge A temporary connecting piece of land between two continents, which allows people and animals to pass across.

latitude Distance in degrees north or south of the equator.

lava The molten rock that flows out of a volcano and then solidifies.

longitude Distance in degrees east or west of the prime meridian (imaginary line that runs between the poles through Greenwich, London, England).

magma Molten rock within the Earth.

mantle The thick layer of dense rock beneath the Earth's crust or continental plates. It carries heat from the core of the planet and produces volcanic activity on the surface.

monsoon Seasonal wind in Asia that brings heavy rains from the Indian Ocean.

navigation The science of plotting a route and steering a ship along it.

nutrient Foodstuff used by plants and animals.

ocean A very large body of saltwater. The five oceans are: the Atlantic, Pacific, Indian, Arctic, and Antarctic.

peninsula A piece of land projecting into the sea from a larger body of land.

plankton Tiny plants and animals that live in the surface layer of the sea. Plankton is the basis of the ocean's food chain.

plate A huge piece of Earth's rocky crust that slides across its surface in a process called continental drift.

polyp Small tube-shaped animal with tentacles round its mouth.

quota The allowable catch of a fishing vessel. The quota system aims to conserve fish stocks, but is difficult to enforce.

salinity Saltiness.

sea A body of saltwater smaller than an ocean, often enclosed by land, such as the Mediterranean Sea.

seamount Extinct underwater volcano.

sediment Layer of organic deposits on the seabed.

silt Mineral-rich mud that is washed into the sea by rivers.

smoker Underwater chimney made of minerals on the deep seabed. It gushes superheated water.

strait Narrow waterway between two landmasses.

submersible Submarine with crew designed to work deep underwater.

subsistence farming Farming that produces only enough food for the use of the farming family.

tide The regular rise and fall of sea level caused by the gravitational pulls of the Moon and Sun on Earth.

trade winds Winds blowing steadily in one direction, so called because they enabled traders to sail across the ocean.

tsunami Series of huge freak waves caused by an undersea earthquake or volcano.

turbine A machine in which the energy of moving water, steam or air is used to turn blades and drive a generator.

INDEX

Abbreviations: t-top, m-middle, b-bottom, r-right, l-left, c-center
Indexer: Jane Parker   **Artwork credits:** 23ml—Geoff Ball. 28bl, 28/29bm—John Marius Butler. 47tr, 67mr—James Field. 20/21, 23br, 58bl—Piers Harper. 19mr, 31tl, 31mr, 50tr—Terry Riley. All maps, 18bm—Stephen Sweet. 14mr—Mike Taylor.

Photograph credits:
Abbreviations: t-top, m-middle, b-bottom, r-right, l-left, c-center
Cover main, 32tr, 35br, 36b, 44bm, 51ml, 51br, 55c, 56tr, 56br, 66tl, 69br, 73bc, 73bl, 75ml—Corbis. Front cover tm, bl, 1, 2-3, 45tm—Stockbyte. Cover (front: tr, bm, back: ml, mr, br), 17ml, 25tr, 25br, 26br, 27mr, 33br, 34br, 36-37, 43mr, 45tr, 47br, 49mr, 54bl, 54tr, 56bl, 61t, 64bl, 65tr, 68tr, 69ml, 69tr, 75t—Digital Stock. Back cover tr, 60bl, 61c, 64mr—Brian Hunter Smart. 4bl, 50br, 77tr—Peter Turnley/CORBIS. 5tl—Zefa-Stockmarket. 5tr, 59mr, 67b—Wolfgang Kaehler/CORBIS. 5b, 23mr—Jeffrey L. Rotman/CORBIS. 5br, 66br, 73mr—Stephen Frink/CORBIS. 6 both, 31ml, 41t, 41c, 43bl, 62bl. 64t—Bettmann/CORBIS. 7t, 7mr, 34mr, 76tr, 77ml—National Maritime Museum Picture Library. 7bl, 7c, 46bl, 47tl—Hulton-Deutsch Collection/CORBIS. 7br—Select Pictures. 10, 11 both, 24ml, 73ml—The Natural History Museum. 12bl—H D Brandl/FLPA-Images of Nature. 12tr—Elio Ciol/CORBIS. 13ml, 19br, 52mr, 71tl, 71br, 74tr—David Hosking/FLPA-Images of Nature. 14b, 61bl, 68-69—Stockbyte. 15ml—Yann-Arthus-Bertrand/CORBIS. 15tr both—L G Nilsson/Skylight/FLPA-Images of Nature. 16tl—FLPA-Images of Nature. 16br all, 17t both, 22mt, 37mr, 38br, 42c, 49br, 51c, 52bl, 65t, 70mr, 76bl—NASA. 22mb—Lester V. Bergman/CORBIS. 22bl—Peter Johnson/CORBIS. 23tl—Kennan Ward/CORBIS. 24mr—Silvestris Photoservice/FLPA-Images of Nature. 27mr—Rick Price/CORBIS. 33ml—PhotoSource. 39ml, 74b—Michael Hollings/FLPA-Images of Nature. 39br—S. Jonasson/FLPA-Images of Nature. 41ml—Phil Claydon/ Eye Ubiquitous/CORBIS. 41br—Rick Tomlinson/Kos Picture Services. 42tr—Winifred Wisniewski/FLPA-Images of Nature. 42bl—Paul Thompson; Eye Ubiquitous/CORBIS. 42br—Charles E. Rotkin/CORBIS. 44bl—Brian Vikander/CORBIS. 45mr—Ian Yates; Eye Ubiquitous/CORBIS. 46br—CORBIS. 47c—The Stock Market. 48mr—Martin Smith/FLPA-Images of Nature. 49ml, 63tl—Roger Tidman/FLPA-Images of Nature. 49bl—GSF Picture Library. 50bl—Richard T. Nowitz/CORBIS. 52ml, 52bm—Barry Lewis/CORBIS. 53mr—Panda Photo/FLPA-Images of Nature. 53ml—Earl & Nazima Kowall/CORBIS. 53br—Richard Bickel/CORBIS. 55ml—Galen Rowell. 55mr—Bob Krist/CORBIS. 55br—Franklin McMahon/CORBIS. 58tr—Jim Richardson/CORBIS. 58br—Kevin Schafer/CORBIS. 59tr—Natalie Fobes/CORBIS. 59bl—Paul A. Souders/CORBIS. 60tr—Nik Wheeler/CORBIS. 61ml—Stephanie Maze/CORBIS. 61br—Lynda Richardson/CORBIS. 63tr—George Lepp/CORBIS. 62br—Mark Newman. 63c — Fritz Polking/FLPA-Images of Nature. 63b—Michael T. Sedman/CORBIS. 65c—Christine Osborne/CORBIS. 65br, 69mr—Jonathon Blair/CORBIS. 65ml—A.N.T./NHPA. 66ml—Historical Picture Archive/CORBIS. 67mt—Dave G. Houser/CORBIS. 67tr—Tony Arruza/CORBIS. 70bl—John Foxx Images. 72br—Derek Hall/FLPA-Images of Nature. 73tl—Adam Woolfitt/CORBIS. 75tr—Sergio Dorantes/CORBIS. 75br—Christophe Loviny/CORBIS. 76br—Trevor MacDonald/NHPA. 77br—Bojan Brecelj/CORBIS.